OP

150

DÜRER

and his world

DÜRER

and his world

BY MAX STECK

A STUDIO BOOK

THE VIKING PRESS · NEW YORK

Dürer: Eine Bildbiographie
© Copyright 1957 by Kindler Verlag Munchen
Translated from the German by J. Maxwell Brownjohn
© Copyright 1964 by Thames and Hudson, Ltd., London
Published in 1964 by The Viking Press, Inc.
625 Madison Avenue, New York, N. Y. 10022
Library of Congress catalog card number 64-12234
Printed in Austria

Earliest-known view of Nuremberg (1483) on the *Krell Altar-piece* in the Lorenzkirche

ALBRECHT DÜRER's celebrated self-portrait in a fur-trimmed coat originated in the year 1500. At about the same period, the free community into which Dürer had been born attained its prime and enjoyed the prosperity which won the free imperial city of Nuremberg its reputation as the loveliest medieval city in the Empire. It was to Nuremberg that Dürer's father, Albrecht Dürer the Elder, had moved as a young man from Hungary in order to learn the goldsmith's craft from Hieronymus Holper, who later became his father-in-law. Dürer's family came from the vicinity of the modern town of Grosswardein, and can be traced back to his grandfather Anthoni Dürer or Türer. The family's name *(Tür* is a German translation of the Hungarian *eytas,* meaning 'door') prompted them to use an open door on their coat of arms and seal. Dürer compiled a 'family chronicle' from his father's papers, a moving but virtually neglected document which tells of his life and background.

Dürer's Hungarian origins

'I, Albrecht Dürer the Younger, have put together from my father's writings whence he hailed, how he came hither, remained here and went to his salvation. God be merciful to him and us. Amen.

His father

'Albrecht Dürer the Elder was born of a family in the Kingdom of Hungary, not far from a small township named Gyula, eight miles below Wardein, in a

5

Dürer's Coat of Arms. Woodcut, 1523

little village near at hand, Eytas by name, and his family kept oxen and horses for a living.

'My father's father was named Anthoni Dürrer; he went as a boy to a goldsmith in the said township and learned the craft from him. Thereafter he wedded a young woman named Elisabetha, who bore him a daughter, Katharina, and three sons. The first son, Albrecht Dürrer by name, was my beloved father, who also became a goldsmith, a chaste and skilful man.

'Thereafter, Albrecht Dürrer, my dear father, came to Germany. He had spent much time with the great artists in the Netherlands, and at last came to Nuremberg on St Eulogius' day, 1455 years after the birth of Christ . . . Then my grandfather gave him 1467 his daughter, a comely and upright maid named Barbara, fifteen years of age. And he wedded her eight days before St Vitus' day. Be it also known that my grandmother, my mother's mother, was the daughter of Oellinger of Weissenburg, and was named Kunigund.'

Dürer's parents married on 6 August 1467. His father was admitted to citizenship of Nuremberg in the same year and acquired his master's status a year later. The couple set up house in the back portion of what is now 20 Winkler-

Dürer's birthplace in Nuremberg
(20 Winklerstrasse, now destroyed)

strasse, which belonged to the parents of Willibald Pirckheimer, Dr Johannes Pirckheimer and his wife Barbara, née Löffelholz. It was in this house, which stood near the Herrenmarkt, Nuremberg's main market, that Albrecht Dürer the Younger was born on 21 May 1471. The entry in the family chronicle reads: 'Item, 1471 years after the birth of Christ, at the sixth hour of the day, on St Prudentia's day, a Tuesday in Rogation week, my wife Barbara bore me a second son. Anthoni Koburger stood godfather to him and named him Albrecht, after me.'

According to a letter in Latin addressed to Willibald Pirckheimer and dated 23 May 1507, Dürer's friend Lorenz Beheim subsequently cast his natal horoscope on the basis of the above information.

Dürer's horoscope

'I have, moreover, cast our Albrecht's nativity, which I am also sending him. He will show it to you himself. I believe I have cast it aright, since all tallies so well. He has the Lion in the house of the ascendant, hence he is lean. Because the Wheel of Fortune stands at its end, he earns money, to whit — since Mercury is in the ascendant — on account of his skill at painting. Because, in addition, Mercury is in the House of Venus, he is a fine painter; and because, conversely, Venus is in the House of Mercury, he is an *ingeniosus amator*. But Venus is separated from Saturn, hence they are to some extent opposed — not that this matters. Because Venus turns toward the Moon, which stands beneath a two-bodied sign, for that reason he desires many (women). But the Moon faces the Dragon's Tail, which signifies decline. And because five planets stand in the centre of the sky, for that reason his deeds and works are manifest to all. And because Mars is in Aries, for that reason he takes pleasure in arms; and because he (Mars) is situated in the ninth house, for that reason he is fond of travelling. And because Jupiter is in the House of Substance, for that reason he will never become poor; yet he will have nothing over, for, in its descent, Jupiter stands in Virgo. According to Ptolemy, he will have but one wife, since the Moon is facing none (of the planets); and it is miraculous that he has indeed married but once. What more shall I say? If he were with me, I should have much else to tell him; but let this suffice. Commend me kindly to him . . . Item, according to Ptolemy's opinion in *Centiloquium* 49, Dürer will rule you. For he says that, if the servant's ascending house be the tenth of the master's ascendance, the servant will rule the master.'

According to the entry relating to his birth, Dürer's godfather was the eminent printer and publisher Anton Koberger, whose establishment produced such famous works as *Schedel's Chronicle of the World* and numerous Latin and German editions of the Bible. Nuremberg itself was a South German book-printing centre at this time, and 1543 saw the publication there of a work which still governs our astronomical system today and whose author gave it

its name: Nicolaus Copernicus' *Revolutiones orbium caelestium*.

Dürer's father, who worked as a goldsmith for the city's churches and for Emperor Frederick III, also trained a number of distinguished Nuremberg goldsmiths. His only surviving letter was written to his wife on 24 August 1492, while he was staying in Linz at the Emperor's invitation. The Emperor had called him 'my goldsmith', a fact of which he was extremely proud. Dürer writes of his father in the family chronicle:

Astrological Drawing. Woodcut, 1503/04

'Item, the said Albrecht Dürrer the Elder led a life of great exertion and hard, strenuous toil, gaining a livelihood from nothing other than that which he earned for himself, his wife and child with his own hand; so that he owned little enough... He also won just repute among those that knew him, for he led an honourable Christian life, was a patient and gentle man, friendly disposed toward all and steadfastly thankful to God. He had, moreover, little use for company and worldly pleasures, being of few words and a God-fearing man.

'My dear father took great pains with his children, to rear them in the fear of God. For his greatest desire was that he should bring up his children well, so that they might please both God and men. Wherefore he enjoined us daily to love God and deal faithfully with our neighbours.'

Of Dürer's mother, who survives only in the marvellous drawing dated 1514, the chronicle has this to say:

'For she had no easy time after my father's death (1502). It was her custom to spend much time at church, and she always upbraided me roundly if I behaved ill. And she was always much exercised over my own and my brothers'

'Schöner Brunnen' and Frauenkirche, Nuremberg

sins. Whether I went out or came in, her constant admonition was: "Go in the name of Christ!" She never wearied of holy exhortations and was ever concerned for our souls. And I cannot sufficiently praise her good works, the compassion which she showed toward all, and her good reputation. My pious mother bore and reared eighteen children. She often had the Plague and many other grave and severe ailments, suffered great poverty, scorn, derision, insulting words, terror and great adversity; yet she never bore malice.' *His mother*

Dürer had numerous brothers and sisters, most of whom died at an early age. 1484 saw the birth of his brother Endres, whom he portrayed several times and also used as a model. Endres, who worked as a goldsmith in

9

Dürer's Father. Silverpoint drawing made at the age of fifteen

Only extant letter from Dürer's father, written to his wife in 1492 to inform her that Emperor Frederick III had named him 'his goldsmith'

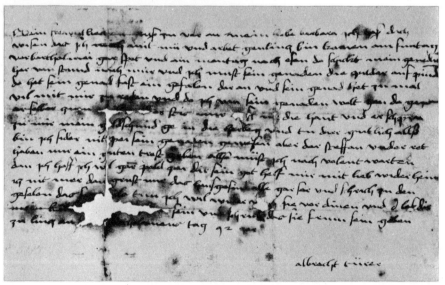

Dürer's Mother. Drawing dated 1514 and inscribed: 'This is Albrecht Dürer's mother; she was 63 years old.' (Addendum) 'And passed away in the year 1514 on the Tuesday before Rogation week at two o'clock in the night'

Entry relating to Endres Dürer's registration as a
master-goldsmith in the official records of Nuremberg.
The Latin text reads: 'Hans Sidlman and Endres Dürer
were sworn on the 3rd (day) after Martinmas 1514
(14 November) / Sidlman gave x Gulden'

Dürer's brother Endres. Drawing, 1514, with the handwritten addendum: 'Endres Dürer was drawn thus
when he was thirty years old'

25–21 Burgstrasse, Nuremberg, showing the houses of
Dürer senior and Michael Wolgemut. Extreme right:
Dürer's parental home. Third from right: Wolgemut's
house

Nuremberg, took over his father's workshop on his death and became a master in 1514. The seventeenth birth recorded in the family chronicle was that of Hanns Dürer, who became a painter and illustrator, and received his training in Albrecht's studio. Apparently, he was a difficult youth and a constant source of worry to his mother. He later worked in Cracow as Court painter to the King of Poland.

Willibald Pirckheimer, the son of the Dürers' landlord, was born a year before Albrecht in the immediate vicinity of the Herrenmarkt. The two boys grew up together, and their childhood friendship blossomed into a lifelong attachment. In 1475, Dürer senior and his large family moved into a house of their own at the intersection of upper Schmiedgasse and Burgstrasse, near St Sebald's church. This was the house known as 'Unter der Vesten', where Dürer's father established his goldsmith's workshop. His neighbour, who lived only two doors away, was the painter Michael Wolgemut. The house stood in the so-called Latin quarter af Nuremberg, and Schedel, Scheurl and other humanists lived close by. Dürer was four years old when the move to the new house took place. His father, who came to regard him more and more as his favourite son, sent him to St Lorenz grammar-school and later trained him as a goldsmith.

Dürer's brother Hanns. Drawing dated 1503 and inscribed: 'I was drawn thus; I was some (?) years old. Hanns Dürer'

Self-portrait at the age of thirteen. Silverpoint drawing with the handwritten addendum: 'I drew myself from a mirror in the year 1484, when I was still a child. Albrecht Dürer'

'And my father took especial pleasure in me, for he saw that I was industrious and eager to learn. For that reason he sent me to school, and, when I had learnt to read and write, took me away from the school and taught me the goldsmith's craft.

Apprenticeship 'But, when I could work neatly, my fancy inclined me more to painting than to goldsmith's work. I put this to my father, but he was not well content, for he regretted the time lost while I had been learning the goldsmith's craft. Nevertheless, he yielded to me, and on St Andrew's day, 1486 years after Christ's birth, my father bound me apprentice to Michael Wolgemut, to serve him three years long. During that time God granted me diligence, so that I learnt well, though I had to endure much from his lads (apprentices and journeymen).'

Michael Wolgemut was a reputable artist with a command of all branches of painting and contemporary techniques. His principal work was probably the altar-piece in St Jacob's church at Straubing, which originated in about 1475. Discernible in the landscape background are the pentagonal tower and watchtower of Nuremberg's fortress, still without the imperial stables. In Wolgemut's

Wing of the altar-piece in St Jacob's, Straubing, *c.* 1475, principal work of Michael Wolgemut. (In the background, the pentagonal tower and watchtower of Nuremberg Castle, as yet without the royal stables)

Michael Wolgemut, portrait dated 1516 and inscribed: 'Albrecht Dürer made this likeness of his master Michell Wolgemut in the year 1516.' (Addendum) 'And he was 82 years old and lived until the year 1519, when he passed away on St Andrew's day, early, before the sun rose'

View of Nuremberg and the imperial forest. Watercolour, 1516

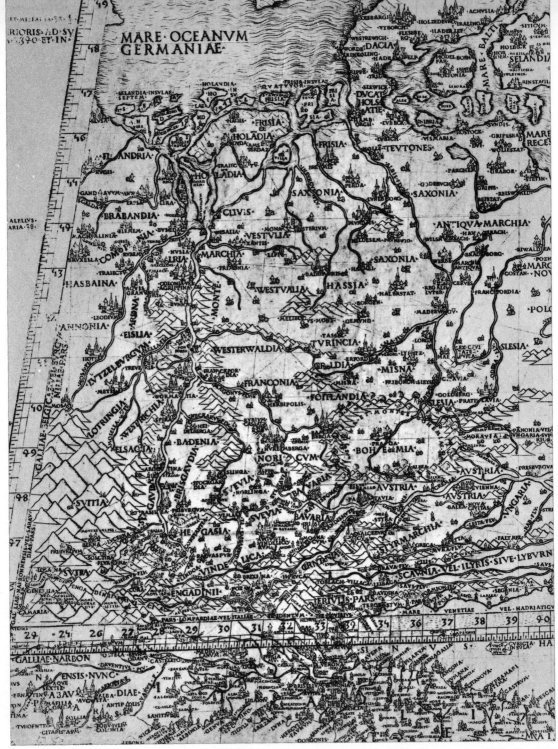

Detail from the map of the world by Nikolaus Cusanus, printed at Eichstätt, 1491

Madonna in a Courtyard
by Martin Schongauer. Copperplate

atelier, the young Dürer was trained primarily to become a competent draughtsman, but he also acquired a thorough grounding in woodcut engraving and painting. His term of apprenticeship expired in the spring of 1490. Dürer senior wanted his nineteen-year-old son to see something of the world, and planned that he should receive further training in the Rhineland and the Netherlands, where he himself had acquired his main artistic impressions and style of craftsmanship some forty years earlier. Martin Schongauer's copperplate engravings, with their fine lines engraved in metal, had captured young Albrecht's imagination. He decided to become a copperplate engraver like his idol, beside whose delicately articulated Rhenish elegance his own work and that of the Nuremberg painters and woodcut engravers seemed clumsy and uncouth.

Albrecht Dürer set out from Nuremberg early in 1490, after Easter, but he

His travels in the Upper Rhine area

did not arrive in Colmar, where Schongauer had his atelier, until more than a year later. History does not relate where he spent the intervening period, but it may have been the Netherlands. On arrival at Colmar, the young man experienced his first great disappointment. The venerable man whose pupil he had wanted to become was dead, having died some months earlier at Breisach on the other side of the Rhine, where he had devoted his waning energies to completing the murals for his *Last Judgement.* However, Martin's brothers, who were carrying on his studio, cordially welcomed the young journeyman from Nuremberg. The copperplate engravings with their gleaming tracery of lines and 'MS' monograms, which Dürer handled daily, must have fascinated him, for he tried to emulate their slim, elegant curves, their modishly graceful figurative poses and calligraphic flourishes of clothing and drapery. His personal style of drawing changed, acquiring brilliance and tonality. He poured out his love of decoration and goldsmith's delicacy of touch into his figures. His drawings of young men, whether standing or walking, invariably had a

The Temptation of St Anthony by Martin Schongauer. Copperplate

Self portrait (1493) holding a thistle. The painting bears Dürer's handwritten note: 'My fortunes fare as it is written above'

Christ-Child with Globe. Tempera on parchment, 1493

hint of the self-portrait about them which mirrored the growing self-awareness of a twenty-year-old who was taking his first steps in the world. Then again, Dürer would be overwhelmed by a mood of gloomy uncertainty. It must have been at such a time that he carelessly turned over a saint's picture and drew his own reflexion on the reverse, a youth with a questioning, profoundly melancholy expression, his face half hidden by one hand, his brooding eyes filled with a look of self-inquiry. No Western artist had ever subjected himself to such grave and intensive scrutiny.

Dürer's subsequent self-portraits always had the same self-awareness. As an artist, he was conscious of himself and his vocation. This trait recurs in the famous Munich self-portrait; stern, composed and not devoid of vanity. Yet, some while earlier, in 1493, he portrayed himself in velvet and silk, a grave, handsome young man who already suggests the *ingeniosus amator* of his horoscope. Significantly, he is holding a species of thistle in his hand, a medieval symbol of masculine fidelity. Could the picture have been intended as a gift for the future bride whom his father had already found for him at home? The rhyme beside the date (1493) — *My sach die gat als es oben schtat* ('My fortunes fare as it is written above') — betrays Dürer's deep religious faith.

View of Basle. Woodcut from *Schedel's Chronicle of the World*, Nuremberg 1493

After spending some months in Colmar with the brothers Ludwig, Paulus and Kaspar Schongauer, Dürer made for Basle, then a major printing centre and a place where leading publishers employed numerous woodcut engravers to illustrate their books. Dürer, who must have had excellent references from his godfather Koberger to the printing houses of Amerbach and Kessler, found work there without difficulty. A letter which he wrote to Amerbach fifteen years later, when he was already a celebrated artist, refers to his time in Basle. 'To the esteemed, wise Master Hanns, book-printer in the small town of Basle, my dear master: first, my humble duty to you, dear Master Hanns. Your fortunate condition is an especial joy to me, who wish you happiness and prosperity, and all those whom you wish well, and especially your esteemed wife, whom I wish well with all my heart. If it please you, write to me of what good thing you are doing now, and forgive me for obliging you to read my artless letter. And so, many good nights. Given at Nuremberg, 1507, 20 October. Albrecht Dürer.'

Wood-block for *St Jerome*, signed '*Albrecht Dürer von nörmergk*' (Nuremberg) on reverse

St Jerome removing the Thorn from the Lion's Paw. Woodcut, 1492

Dürer earned his living in Basle as a woodcut engraver — a commercial artist, as we should term it nowadays. In addition, he drew illustrations, initials and marginal decoration for the woodcuts in books produced by Basle's famous printing houses. Generally speaking, Dürer only made working drawings for woodcuts. His celebrated sets of woodcut engravings were not engraved by him personally. On the other hand, he may also have done some actual engraving in Basle, because there is one woodcut extant *(St Jerome removing the Thorn from the Lion's Paw)* which bears the note 'Albrecht Dürer of Nuremberg' on the reverse.

Facsimile of a letter from Dürer to the printer Amerbach of Basle, dated 20 October 1507

Self-portrait with Cushion. Pen-drawing, 1493

It is certain that Dürer also worked on the illustrations in Sebastian Brant's *Ship of Fools,* and some experts have recognized his hand in an illustrated edition of Terence published at Basle in the 'nineties. The whole of Basle's book-printing output during these years was pervaded by a luxuriance of form and artistic vitality which is attributable to Dürer's influence and which disappeared after his departure. It was not until twenty years later, when the Latin and Greek classics and the New Testament were edited by the Rotterdam scholar Erasmus and illustrated by the eighteen-year-old artist Hans Holbein the Younger, that book-printing attained a comparable standard.

Where else the young Franconian artist's *Wanderjahre* (1490—94) took him remains obscure. Did he spend a short time with Mantegna in northern Italy at this period, or was his familiarity with the classic lucidity of that artist's relief compositions, in which he found what he still lacked, based on the odd few engravings that happened to pass through his hands? Mantegna's name drew Dürer to Italy. Nuremberg lay far away in the past. New horizons were unfolding. A Genoese sailor had attempted to reach India by the westward route and had, so it was said, discovered an immense continent: America. Having lain fallow for a millennium and a half, the soil of Italy was bringing forth an art of infinite purity and greatness. Artists were being summoned to share in a revival, a renascence — a 're-awakening', as Dürer put it. He eagerly snapped up each fresh report, each new evidence of it. A new world was opening its doors. The confines of his Franconian past lay behind him, and his gaze was focused on what lay ahead.

His marriage   Then news arrived from Nuremberg which was to exercise a decisive influence on the course of his life. He was summoned home to marry a bride whom he had never seen — Agnes Frey, the young daughter of a locally respected man. The marriage had been arranged by the couple's parents. Hanns Frey, Dürer's future father-in-law, was an inventive, humorous man who loved

Martin Behaim's 'earth-apple', or globe (1490–92)

Map by Hieronymus Münzer from *Schedel's Chronicle of the World*, Nuremberg 1493

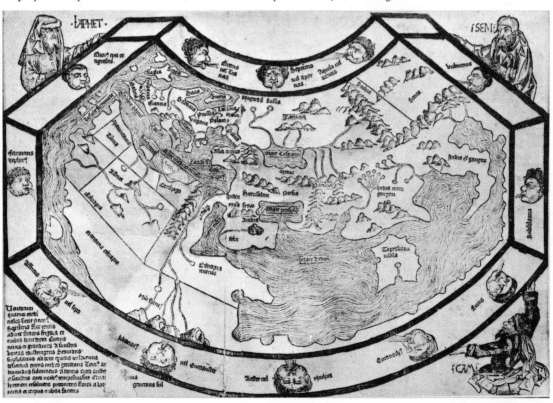

music as much as Dürer did himself. He was a business man and a *'mechanicus'* after the style of Peter Henlein, the inventor of the pocket-watch. He was also steward of the Rathaus of Nuremberg and became a 'nominee of the Grand Council' shortly after his daughter's marriage.

Dürer senior had arranged what seemed in every respect an advantageous match for his son. Agnes brought with her a dowry of 200 gulden — enough

Lady of Nuremberg in Church-going Dress

Lady of Nuremberg in Ball-dress.
Pen-drawings with water-colour, 1500

to buy a house in those days — and could look forward to inheriting a substantial sum later on. In May 1494 Dürer, now twenty-three, arrived from the south-west, and on 7 July of the same year he married her.

Although he wrote 'My Agnes' on a drawing of his wife dating from the early days of their marriage, that was the only tender word which Dürer,

My Agnes.
Pen-drawing of the
artist's wife, 1494–95

Venice. Woodcut from *Schedel's Chronicle of the World*, Nuremberg 1493

who made so many solicitous and affectionate remarks about his father, mother and family in his diaries, jottings and letters, ever accorded her. His childless state lay like a dark shadow across his life.

A few months after his marriage, Dürer again set off on his travels, not least because of the Plague, which had broken out in Nuremberg and was daily claiming hundreds of victims. By Christmas 1494, only 17,000 of the town's former population of 25,000 were still alive. Those aristocrats and prominent citizens who could escape to the country did so, but Dürer would have had nothing to do there. While he may have been lured to Italy by thoughts of Mantegna's engravings, the final impetus was given by his friends Pirckheimer and Scheurl, who had both studied at Padua. Nuremberg maintained a trading agency in Venice, which was near Padua, so there would be friends and fellow-countrymen there as well as great artists.

His first visit to Italy   In September 1494, Albrecht Dürer travelled down the old trade route and pilgrim's road which led, via Eichstätt, Augsburg, Schongau, Mittenwald, Innsbruck and the Brenner, to the South. The couriers employed by the Augsburg and Nuremberg merchants who maintained a postal service of their own with the German trading establishment by the Rialto Bridge in Venice, the *fondaco dei tedeschi,* took about ten days to complete the trip. Dürer's journey on foot took roughly three times as long, but in the course of it he found — without looking for it — the thing which was to make his place in European painting so unique: his feeling for landscape.

The harmonious landscape backgrounds for his saints and Madonnas had hitherto been provided by the gentle Franconian hills. He had collected

Detail from *Etzlaub's Map* (1492), on which Dürer's route to Venice can be traced ▶

View of Innsbruck from the north. Water-colour, 1494

material for such backgrounds in the vicinity of Nuremberg, fighting a running battle with perspective, which he had failed to master entirely in *The Wire-Drawing Mill or The Little Church of St John,* and which formed his principal reason for visiting Italy. Few at that time thought of water-colours as pictures in their own right or of landscape as a valid pictorial theme in itself, least of all Dürer, whose lofty conception of the mission and purpose of art — 'art is of value when God is honoured thereby' — grew firmer with every passing year. For all that, his journey on foot took him through unfamiliar scenery, and hand and eye could scarcely keep up with the flood of new impressions. His object was less to paint pictures than to make sketches which might prove useful later on.

With a gift of observation and a sensitivity to his natural surroundings which were not to recur until the advent of the nineteenth-century Romanticists, Corot or the great French Impressionists, Dürer drank in the colour of the countryside, the violet haze on the sides of southward-facing valleys in the southern Tyrol, the silvery green of the olive groves at the foot of the fortress of Arco, the stronghold north of Lake Garda, at the extremity of the Venetian sphere of influence. The painter awoke in a draughtsman who spent a lifetime reducing what he saw to the stern discipline of linear representation. Dürer was, in fact, a brilliantly talented painter — perhaps the greatest in the history of German art — but he austerely renounced the explosive, expressive power of colour in favour of pure form.

More than a dozen sketch-book sheets have survived from Dürer's journey on foot through the Alps. One water-colour of Innsbruck depicts the walls and towers of the town reflected in the gleaming, grey-blue waters of the Inn, with the Patscherkofel in the background.

The *Hinterburg* of Innsbruck Castle was occupied by Maximilian, later Emperor Maximilian I but at that time King of Germany and ruler of the Tyrol. Dürer made a water-colour of the castle courtyard, but he did not meet his future patron and protector personally on this occasion. Once again, perspective gave Dürer so much trouble that he essayed the same view twice.

Courtyard of the Hinterburg at Innsbruck, water-colour, 1494. (Residence of Dürer's patron, later Emperor Maximilian I)

Nemesis
('The Great
Fortune').
Copperplate,
c. 1501, with view
of Chiuso in the
Tyrol

View of Trento from the north. Water-colour, 1494/95

On the way across the Brenner, Dürer recorded the Eysacktal near Klausen, which he later used in the copperplate engraving *Nemesis*. Trento, valleys in the southern Dolomites, a water-mill, a tumbledown castle on a steep crag above the river — water-colours such as these enable one to trace Dürer's journey to Venice with some accuracy. He arrived there in October 1494. The *fondaco dei tedeschi*, the German trading centre and club-house near the Rialto Bridge, became his centre of operations during his stay.

One hundred thousand people lived in the lagoon-city beside the Adriatic at this period, four times as many as lived within the walls of Dürer's native Nuremberg. He had arrived in a metropolis which dominated the entire eastern half of the Mediterranean, both economically and — since its acquisition of the Crusaders' island of Cyprus — militarily. Venice was the place where Turks, Negroes, Indians, trade missions from Byzantium and Baghdad, ships from Arabia, envoys from Sultan Soliman — the whole of the Orient in all its rich variety — debouched on to the shores of Europe. And Venice herself, Queen of the

Venetian Lady. Pen-drawing and wash, 1495

Seas, entertained her guests with processions, festivals and gorgeous spectacles. The haste with which Dürer filled his sketch-books — studies in oriental physiognomy, copies of mythological scenes, and sketches of women's fashions jostle one another on the same sheet — only illustrates what a wealth of impressions must have crowded in upon the artist. The Piazza San Marco, the Piazzetta, the Riva degli Schiavoni, where ships unloaded and dealers displayed their wares, must have seemed like an oriental bazaar, full of a thousand marvels. Dürer drew lions and snakes, Moslems in long caftans, half-naked Saracens and beturbaned Turks mounted on nimble Arab steeds. Apart from the colourful turmoil of the squares, alley-ways and canals, Dürer was fascinated by marine life — lobsters, cuttle-fish and crabs — and reproduced the unfamiliar sea-creatures displayed on fishmongers' counters with zoological accuracy. As for the ladies of the city with their precious damasks, lace veils and daring

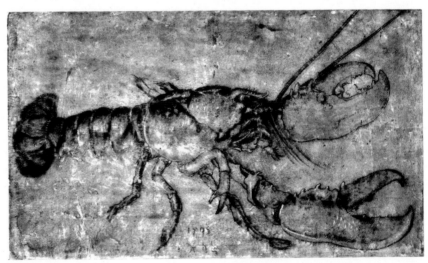

The Lobster.
Tempera, 1495

The Whore of Babylon. Woodcut from *The Apocalypse,* 1498

Virgin and Child. Chalk, 1518/19   *The Great Hercules.* Copperplate, c. 1500

décolletages — a few years later he was ungallant enough to use a drawing of an aristocratic Venetian lady as a model for *The Whore of Babylon,* a woodcut in the *Apocalypse* series. Back home, with the good women of Nuremberg before his eyes once more, such refined habits of dress and behaviour must have struck him as the very embodiment of sinful and seductive charm.

Mantegna was the magic word which had lured Dürer to Italy, yet little of the austere grandeur which characterized the rediscovery of classical antiquity could be detected in the metropolis on the Adriatic, where the glittering golden Gothic mingled with the variegated splendour of the Orient. Through the good offices of the painter Gentile Bellini, who happened to be Mantegna's brother-in-law, Dürer managed to get a sight of some of Mantegna's Roman subjects. He copied them, but even Antonio Pollaiuolo's mythological scenes were of a porcelain-like fragility which did not fundamentally satisfy him, although he copied them, too, and used them as an aid to understanding the articulation and proportions of the nude body.

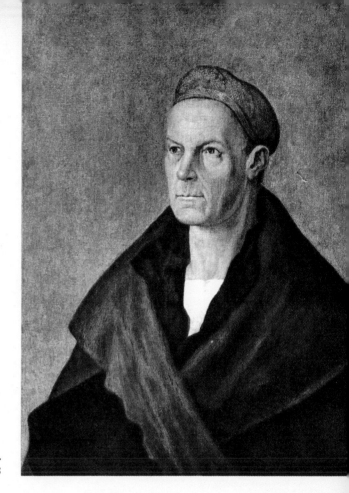

Jakob Fugger ('the Rich').
Oils, *c.* 1518

When Dürer copied a Mantegna engraving it became, under his hands, something different, less significant, more intricate, more exact — perhaps richer. However, he did not see this. He became increasingly convinced that great Italian painters like Mantegna and Leonardo must work according to secret rules and laws. Only this could explain their grandeur, simplicity and clarity of form. Dürer searched for the secret formula like an alchemist searching for the philosopher's stone. He made vain inquiries all over Venice. The kindly Bellini, who had taken to his young fellow-painter from Germany, gave him drawings with exotic subjects but could supply no answer to a question which for him, a Southerner to whom form came naturally, could not have been of such fundamental importance.

Dürer continued to hunt for treatises on art, formulae, books of rules, manuals on proportion — anything which might impart the secret, — but in vain. Then he met a painter in Venice who talked about art in a way which particularly enthralled him. From many of his allusions, Dürer gained the

Venice. Woodcut by Jacopo de'Barbari, the so-called Kolb city-plan, 1500. Probably produced

...ollaboration with Dürer, whose hand has been identified in the wind-gods and the distant Alpine panorama

Sketch-book Sheet, including a 'Rape of Europa'. Pen-drawings, 1494/95

impression that this painter — Jacopo de'Barbari — must have the key to the enigma. 'Yet I found no one who had written of any such thing save one man, Jakobus by name, a good, amiable painter, born in Venice, who showed me the figures of a man and woman which he had drawn in proportion'. But not even he could impart the vital 'foundation', rule or law.

The two men probably got to know one another while collaborating on the large map of Venice which had been commissioned from de'Barbari by the Nuremberg entrepreneur and cloth merchant Anton Kolb. Kolb's map, a cartographic marvel, gave an oblique bird's-eye view of the entire city of Venice,

Apollo. Reversed drawing based on an Italian engraving of the Apollo of Belvedere

Globe.
Woodcut, 1515

showing every house and alley-way, canal and bridge. It was engraved on eight wood-blocks which produced a vast sheet measuring, when the eight sheets were pasted together, some $4^{1}/_{2}$ feet by 9. For publishing this map, which was to be printed at Nuremberg, the Signoria granted Kolb a long-term concession in the city. For decades after its appearance in 1500, this gigantic woodcut remained the standard street plan for any European business man who had dealings with Venice and needed to know every alley-way in the city, and no business establishment on either side of the Alps was without a copy.

Dürer may well have collaborated on the drawings, for his style has been identified in the distant Alpine ranges and the puffed cheeks of the wind-gods. It would have been bread-and-butter work of the sort which he had previously done in Basle. The main result, however, was his encounter with de'Barbari, whom he met again in Nuremberg a few years later and who was known there

Double sheet drawn by Dürer for his friend Johannes Stabius, Court astronomer to Emperor Maximilian

— in his capacity as Court painter to Emperor Maximilian and later to Frederick the Wise, Elector of Saxony, at Wittenberg — as Jakob Walch ('Jacob the Italian'). From Wittenberg, de'Barbari moved to the Netherlands, where the Emperor's daughter, Margaret of Habsburg, had offered him a post as Court painter.

As long as twenty-six years after their first encounter in Venice, at which he was deceived and disillusioned by de'Barbari, who was by far his artistic inferior, Dürer, by then a world-famous figure patronized by the Emperor and admired by Raphael, still remembered the Venetian with respect and gratitude. At an audience granted him by the Regent Margaret during his trip to the Netherlands in 1521, he begged to be given de'Barbari's sketch-book. He was still searching for the golden rule, for examples of the human form 'done in proportion'.

Battle of Tritons. Pen-drawing after Mantegna, 1494

Orpheus Slain by the Thracian Women.
Pen-drawing, 1494 ▶

The Fortress of Arco,
South Tyrol.
('Fenedier Klausen')
Water-colour, 1495

Dürer spent a good six months in Venice, absorbing a wealth of images and impressions, but he never actually found a satisfactory answer to the problem which had brought him there.

In February 1495 he travelled back to Nuremberg, this time probably not through the *welsch pirg* ('Italian mountains' or Dolomites), as one of his water-colours is entitled, but via the Po valley and Lake Garda. Dürer's water-colour of the mountain fortress of Arco, which is assumed to have been painted on the return journey, is like a parting glimpse of the South. *Fenedier Klausen,* he wrote at the head of the sheet — here the Venetian domain ends. It had the ring of a last farewell.

Back in Nuremberg On his return to Nuremberg, Dürer at first lived in his father's house in Burgstrasse, where his young wife was awaiting him. He did some more work

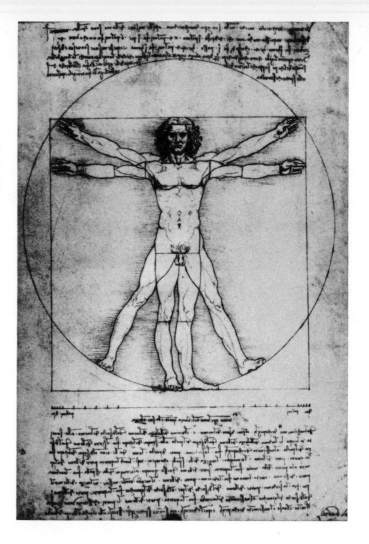

Canon of Human Proportion
by Leonardo da Vinci, after Vitruvius.
Drawing with description in Leonardo's
handwriting (mirror-script)

for Wolgemut, but now found it harder to fit into his old master's atelier. The others failed to understand what inspired him and what had, since Venice, become so much more urgent and disquieting. He needed a studio of his own, a place where he could draw, think, construct and grope his way toward a solution of his problems. Nature was fashioned 'in proportion' — i. e. in accordance with immutable laws — and the same had to apply to art. Dürer was looking for a comprehensive formula which embraced truth and beauty alike.

There was only one person with whom Dürer could discuss all these questions — not a painter, but someone who knew Italy, had studied at Padua and spent some time in Venice, someone who had a verbal appreciation of the grand, simple rhythm which Dürer was seeking to realize in visual terms and who could discourse enthusiastically on the writers and philosophers of Greece

Ornamental Knot
by a pupil of Leonardo
da Vinci

View of Nuremberg
by Hans Wurm.
Water-colour, *c.* 1520

Willibald Pirckheimer.
Charcoal-drawing, 1503

49

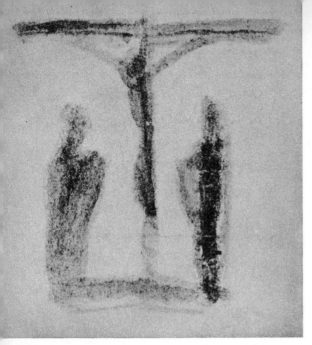

Miraculous Cross. A memento of the Plague epidemic in Nuremberg, 1503

and Rome. Willibald Pirckheimer, young and scholarly scion of a prosperous patrician family, was a year older than Dürer. The Pirckheimers had lived in Nuremberg for generations, although Willibald's father had spent some time in Eichstätt as lawyer to the local bishop. Albrecht and Willibald had known each other well as children, having spent their youth almost under the same roof. Now, on this return from Italy, Dürer sought out the young humanist — though it is just conceivable that they had met in Italy, and that Pirckheimer had taken Dürer with him to visit the Sforzas' Court, where Leonardo and Bramante were working at the time. Be that as it may, their renewed acquaintanceship flowered into a lifelong friendship. Dürer initially felt a trifle inferior to the brilliantly gifted, robustly vital patrician's son, who enjoyed great success as a diplomat, poet, senior officer in Nuremberg's municipal forces, as negotiator with the Emperor and princes and, last not least, as an admirer of beautiful women. It was not until his second visit to Venice in 1506, which was to bring Dürer, the craftsman's son, renown and success, that he finally overcame his sense of inferiority. He drew Pirckheimer twice in 1503, once in silverpoint and once in charcoal, but it is also possible that the bizarre engraving entitled *The Doctor's Dream,* made just before the turn of the century, is a disguised portrait and, hence, an allusion to Pirckheimer's gout, which has driven the tireless philanderer to take refuge behind the tiled stove. The Devil is blowing an erotic dream into his ear with a pair of bellows and has conjured up the image of a seductive, naked beauty whom Dürer constructed 'in proportion' and in accordance with all the contemporary canons of beauty.

On the other hand, Dürer may have been using this rebus to poke fun at his friend's 'French disease', an ailment which was one of the greatest banes of a period pervaded by dark unrest. It was the eve of the Reformation. The Empire was disintegrating, the peasants were in revolt, and interminable processions of pilgrims wound their way through the country-side. People had been smitten by a craze for miracles, and crosses were falling from the sky all over Germany. Dürer himself reported in 1503 that a neighbour's servant-girl had been the subject of one of thease miraculous apparitions and believed her end to be imminent. The towns were being depopulated by epidemics of Plague. Far away in the East, the Turkish menace was growing. Constantinople had

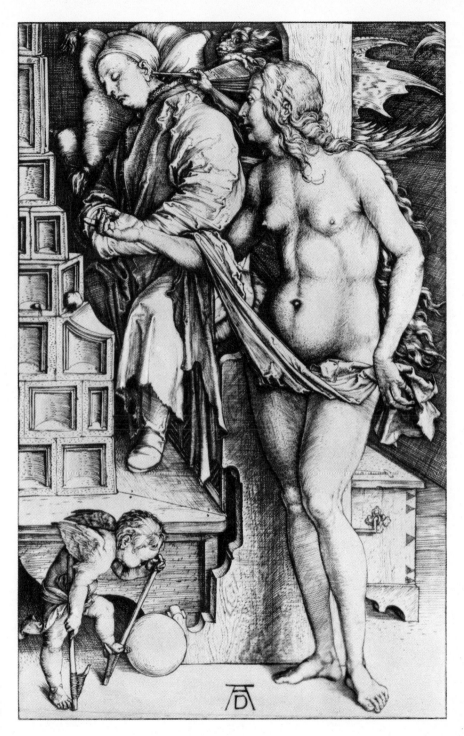

The Doctor's Dream.
Copperplate,
1497–99

German title-page from the *Revelation of St John (Apocalypse)*. Woodcut, 1498

already fallen to the Infidel, who was to threaten Vienna itself a few decades later. The infant German printing industry was simultaneously spreading enlightenment and unrest by churning out a stream of tracts and pamphlets. Humanist intellectuals were undermining the old order and religious fanatics exhorting a redeeming belief in the Last Judgement and the end of the world, which was forecast for the end of the half-millennium.

Fresh from the gaiety and glamour of Venice, Dürer was doubly assailed by this oppressive atmosphere. His stay in Italy had affected him profoundly. He knew that his art must take a new course and he could see his goal, but the route to it was obscure. In a period characterized by universal vacillation and doubt he sought a firm foothold, a rule or law by which to work, and in his mood of despondency he held fast to the only thing which was beyond doubt, the only steadfast and enduring value: the word of God.

The Four Horsemen of the Apocalypse. Woodcut, 1498

This was what inspired *The Apocalypse*, a series of woodcuts steeped in the turbulent mood of the time. It was this work which made Dürer's name famous throughout Europe. The fifteen prints were published by Dürer's own establishment in 1498, in two versions, one with a Latin and one with a German biblical text on the reverse of each sheet. A second edition appeared in 1511, printed by Dürer himself. The types for the text came from his godfather Koberger's workshop.

From 1497 onwards, Dürer signed his engravings with the celebrated monogram 'AD', which, after passing through various transitional stages, now assumed its final form and began to gain validity as an artistic trade-mark throughout Europe. In Italy, for instance, Marcantonio Raimondi and others copied his engravings and adorned them with his monogram. However, attempts to confer distinction on engravings by means of the 'AD' monogram were not confined to copies but extended to inferior work, and it was a dispute over copyright which led to Dürer's second visit to Venice in 1505.

Dürer poured all the artistic gifts and technical experience gained in twenty-seven years of existence into the woodcuts which comprise *The Apocalypse*. Experts have identified Italian, Upper Rhenish and German

The Men's Bath.
Woodcut, 1497/98

St Michael fighting the Dragon. Woodcut from *The Apocalypse*, 1498 ▶

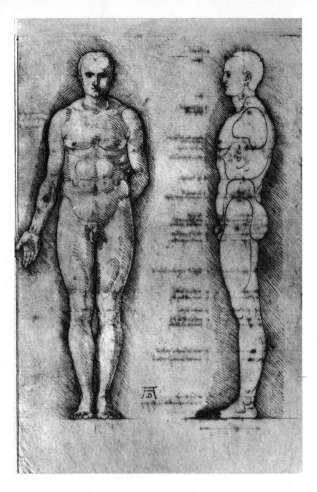

Study in Male Proportion.
Pen-drawing, 1512

elements side by side in his work. He was, to quote his own words, 'inwardly filled with images'. Being uniquely stirred by the visions conjured up by St John's *Revelations,* he was impelled by them to lend expression to his world of imagery.

A period filled with fear and foreboding saw, reflected in these woodcuts, hope and fear, destruction and redemption, judgement and mercy. Between 30 and 40 centimetres high, these almost poster-like prints were not works of art destined for the portfolios of connoisseurs and scholars so much as tracts and challenging sermons for the eye. Not only in form but in content, they summon the beholder to change his way of life.

Dürer was very conscious of his task or mission. His work, from now until the *Four Apostles* of 1526, contains repeated instances of this religious awareness. He felt a need not only to pass on his artistic discoveries and achievements but to proclaim his religious convictions in terms of art. All the series of woodcuts which appeared at about this time are an expression of Albrecht Dürer's attitude toward religion.

The years which intervened between his two trips to Italy were coloured by the dualism and unresolved inquiry implicit in Dürer's personality. His artistic pendulum swung between two extremes. Visionary scenes appeared cheek-by-jowl with gloomy preconceptions about death. The nudes in the copperplate engraving known as *The Four Witches,* in *The Sea-Monster* and *The Doctor's Dream* provide a somewhat cool and rigid illustration of the way in which Dürer accepted Italian art as an academic criterion, although their contours and the thematic content of his engravings are occasionally imbued with genuine and animated sensuality. There is often something touchingly schoolboyish about the unqualified enthusiasm with which he accepted Italian models, copied and elaborated them and incorporated them

Hercules and the Birds of Stymphalis. Oils, 1500

in his own work. Anyone who is tempted to ask whether he impaired his own originality by such an acceptance should study *Hercules and the Birds of Stymphalis.* In this painting, Dürer lifted the figure of the archer-hero from a prototype by Pollaiuolo, translated it into his own idiom — and enhanced it.

For his copperplate engraving *Adam and Eve* (1504), Dürer employed a drawing of Apollo which he had once made from a copy of the Apollo of Belvedere, constructing his figures 'with compass and ruler'. Inspired by his faith in classical art, he translated Apollo into Adam with a faithful regard for the stiff and statuesque quality of the original.

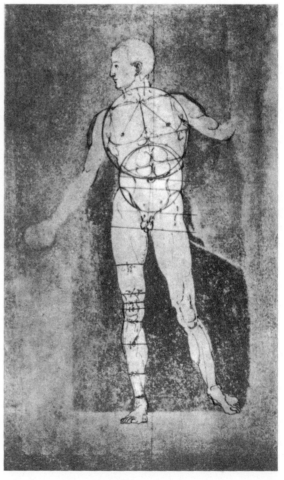

Constructional sketches for
Adam and Eve, 1503/04

Columbine.
Water-colour, *c.* 1502

The still-life-like sheen of a bird's plumage, the warmth of a hare's fur, the subdued glow of violet petals, the rich green of dandelion leaves and the tufted luxuriance of wild grasses — Dürer sensed the radiant warmth inherent in material objects and reproduced it as no German artist had ever done. The network of meshed lines in his copperplate engravings became varied and eloquent so that the smoothness of a bare arm, the horny hardness of a hoof, the metallic sheen of armour could be visually 'felt'.

Success came early to Dürer, and he soon severed the restraining ties that

The Owlet.
Water-colour, 1508

bound him to his master, Wolgemut. In 1497 he established a workshop of his own in his father's house in Burgstrasse, where *The Apocalypse* came into being. His brother Hanns, who later became Court painter at Cracow through the good offices of the celebrated wood-carver Veit Stoss, joined him as an apprentice.

Dürer not only concentrated on formal perfection but pierced the superficial 'skin' of material objects. Large commissions came his way. The Tucher family, a clan of Nuremberg patricians, ordered portraits of six of their

number. Another sitter was *Oswolt Krel,* the impetuous young Lindau
merchant with the ardent, irascible gaze, whom Dürer depicted against a
fiery red background. Then the young artist, whose fame was beginning to
spread, received a commission from Frederick the Wise in Wittenberg. He
was to paint an altar-piece for the castle church there. It turned out to be a
picture distinguished by its 'Italian simplicity', painted in tempera. The panel,
which is in a poor state of preservation, has never left Saxony since it was
painted. *Frederick the Wise* also commissioned a portrait of himself and gave
the young master a pupil 'for board and instruction'. An 'Italian' quality is

OSWOLT·KREL

·1499·

likewise detectable even in the austere monumen-
tality of the Elector's portrait. Dürer was greatly
in demand as a portraitist, and the Paumgartners
comissioned a large altar-piece from him which
incorporated full-length portraits of the donor and
his family. Shortly after 1500 a second summons
came from the Elector of Saxony. Assisted by his
Venetian colleague de'Barbari, Dürer executed
some mural paintings for the Castle at Wittenberg. His painting attained glittering heights in
The Adoration of the Magi, another altar-piece
which he also painted for his patron at Wittenberg. Today the centre panel hangs in the Uffizi
in Florence, while the wings are shared between
Frankfurt and Cologne. Visitors to the gallery
who encounter the dewy freshness of Northern
colouring sandwiched between the blander tones
of the South find it a memorable experience.

The new-found success and fame which travelled across the Alps in the Fuggers' convoys
of merchandise temporarily obscured Dürer's
quest for a solution to technical problems. Perhaps he reflected that he had already gone a
long way for a young man of twenty-seven.
The self-portrait of 1498 shows him gazing at
himself in a mirror, a handsome young man,
well-travelled — as the Alpine view through
the window implies — and foppishly dressed as
a Venetian nobleman. However, the costume is
belied by the melancholy of the eyes, which
suggest that outward pomp is only a façade
concealing a profoundly serious mind whose
interests lie elsewhere.

Two years later Dürer took another look at himself in the mirror. If the
1498 picture, now in Madrid, still contains a hint of the romantic coquetry
of youth, the later portrait lends him a slightly intimidating solemnity and
dignity, pathos and self-awareness. Dürer adopted the austere sym-
metry of Christ's image as Redeemer of the World for his own portrait,
unhesitatingly appropriating, in the interests of structural clarity and formal
order, a schematic form which had hitherto been reserved for the most sacred
of subjects. The pyramid of ringlets, the axis formed by the inscriptions

The Dresden Altar-piece, centre panel and wings, *c.* 1496–99

and eyes, the severely framed rectangle of the face — each component of
this pictorial edifice speaks of Dürer's abstract formal urge. Vestiges of Gothic
delicacy are discernible only in the hand grasping the fur, and in the ringlets,
which resemble the finest gold thread. This picture has become one of the
most celebrated self-portraits in the world, 'fervent and severe', as the artist
saw himself and as the world was to see him.

The great series of woodcuts dating from the period between the two Italian journeys, *The Apocalypse,* the prints comprising *The Life of the Virgin*

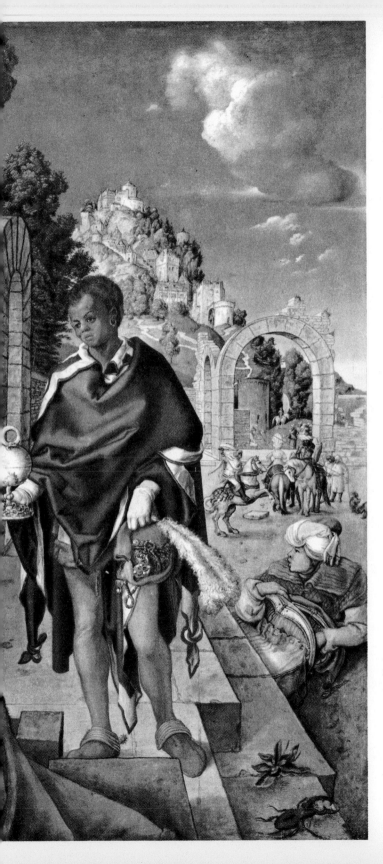

Adoration of the Magi.
Oils, 1504

Stephan Paumgartner, the donor's eldest son, as St George with the Dragon (left-hand panel)

The Paumgartner Altar-piece was installed in the Katharinenkirche, Nuremberg's 'Mastersingers' church', in 1503. The donor of this triptych was Stephan Paumgartner, who placed the commission with Dürer in 1498. In the lower corners of the centre panel, which depicts the Nativity, can be seen the kneeling figures of the donor and his family. Below: the donor's father, Martin Paumgartner, the donor himself and his two sons Lukas and Stephan, who also appear on the side panels in the guise of Christian knights

Female members of the donor's family in the lower right-hand corner of the centre panel: Paumgartner's grandmother, his wife Cordula, *née* Wieland, and one of their daughters. (This altar-piece is now in the Alte Pinakothek, Munich)

Lukas Paumgartner as St Eustace (right-hand panel)

Self-portrait. Oils, 1498. The handwritten inscription reads: 'This I painted after my image. I was twenty-six years old. Albrecht Dürer'

Self-portrait (1500)

and some items from the so-called *Great Passion*, all of 1498, belong together like the movements of a symphony, mutually dependent yet full of contrast.

The year 1502 saw Nuremberg engaged in a bitter feud with Margrave Casimir of Brandenburg. While Casimir was besieging the city and Dürer was, in all probability, helping to defend the ramparts, Albrecht Dürer the Elder died.

Dürer's entry in the family chronicle betrays his consternation. Dürer the Elder died without his son at his side. The old man's wife lit the passing candle and gave him a last drink — Reinfall wine from Rivoglio in Istria, Dürer noted. His father passed away unexpectedly while prayers were being said and he himself was asleep in his room upstairs. 'And the young maid, when she saw the change, ran quickly to my chamber and woke me; but before I came down he had passed away. I saw him dead with great sorrow, for I was unworthy to be with him at his end. Merciful God assist me like-

wise to a blessed end. He left my mother a grieving widow, she whom he had always praised highly to me for being so good a wife; wherefore I undertake never more to forsake her.'

Death had impinged on Dürer's life once again, and its image refused to desert him either as a man or an artist. In 1503 he engraved his strange *Coat of Arms with Skull* on copper. For all its splendour and success, for all its persistent quest for beauty, Dürer's art repeatedly strikes a forlorn note which finds expression, for instance, in his drawing and copperplate engraving *The Prodigal Son*. The unnerving charcoal sketch of 1505 shows a skeleton mounted on an emaciated nag, a scythe in one bony hand and a spiky diadem on its head. In the top left corner is the charcoal inscription *Memento mei*, 'Remember me'. It was a symbol of the Plague, which had once more invaded the countryside in autumn 1505 and was mowing down the population.

Nuremberg became depopulated. Death-carts rumbled through the gates day and night, and the wealthier burghers fled to neighbouring towns, such as Nördlingen and Schwäbisch Gmünd, which had so far been spared.

Dürer hesitated. If he left Nuremberg it could be for only one destination: Italy, where he should have gone long ago to deal with abuses of his name and work by

Latin title-page for *The Life of the Virgin* (woodcut, 1511) and title-page for *The Great Passion* (woodcut, 1510)

The Prodigal Son.
Pen-drawing, 1497/98

Memento mei.
Charcoal drawing, 1505

the engraver Raimondi and sundry others. Italians had been copying his wood-cuts in copperplate, to Dürer's financial and artistic detriment. As before, it was Pirckheimer who decided the issue by lending him the requisite sum to cover travelling expenses. This time, Dürer travelled like a gentleman, complete with horses and a quantity of baggage. It was a far cry from the young journeyman of eleven years before. His baggage included a bale of prints and six small paintings. These he hoped to sell as soon as possible in order to repay his friend's loan, reckoning that in a country where his drawings were so highly prized that people forged them by the score, he was bound to meet with success as a painter. In one of his first letters he was able to inform Pirckheimer that he had already sold four of the six panels. At Augsburg he called a halt in order to visit Konrad Fuchs, a friend of Pirckheimer, who put him in touch with the eminent humanist Konrad Peutinger. Peutinger, who later became known for the 'Peutinger Panel', a map of the world, was clerk of the Fuggers' native city, and it was in Augsburg during September 1505 that Peutinger first broached the subject of the great commission which awaited Dürer in Venice: the altar-piece entitled *The Feast of Rose Garlands* for San Bartolomeo, the German colony's church.

A second visit to Italy   Dürer's route may be deduced from a pair of peasant-women's heads drawn during the trip. *Una vilana windisch* he wrote beside his monogram on the apron of one of the peasants, who smiles broadly at the beholder with narrowed eyes. This drawing may have been made during a halt in some village on the edge of the Alps north of Udine, near the Karawanken, where the local population is still called *windisch* to this day.

Great changes met Dürer in Venice. The German settlement had been burnt down at the beginning of the year and rebuilding was at a standstill because the Signoria refused to allow the Germans any marble for the façade. As it turned out, the architects transformed necessity into a virtue by employing the brilliant young Venetian artist Giorgione to decorate the façade with frescoes, a fragment of which is still preserved as a treasured exhibit in the Academy at Venice. The construction of the new Fondaco had been entrusted to an Augsburg architect named Hieronymus, and it was probably due to Dürer's Augsburg connections that the German business colony commissioned him to produce the altar-piece for San Bartolomeo shortly after his arrival. Dürer showed his appreciation in characteristic fashion by embodying por-traits of the two Augsburgers, Hieronymus and Peutinger, in *The Feast of Rose Garlands*. The contract stipulated that the picture should be completed within five months and mentioned a fee of 110 gulden, which would quickly enable him to settle his debt to Pirckheimer. In a letter dated 6 January 1506 he happily informed his friend that materials would cost him only 5 Gulden and that he would be able to save a tidy sum. His exultation over the large

The Feast of Rose Garlands. Oils, 1506

commission and the honour conferred on him temporarily obscured the fact that life was not cheap in Peter Pander's Gasthof, the leading German hostelry in Venice, which was located conveniently close to San Bartolomeo. Dürer's ten letters to Pirckheimer, which have fortunately survived although the answers are not extant, speak of his joys and cares, his work and the reputation he won during his months in Venice.

Dürer was intensely human. He needed friendship, affection, solicitude. 'I have no other friend on earth but you', he wrote, and: 'I consider you as

Hieronymus of Augsburg
(master-builder). Drawing, 1506

Detail from *The Feast of Rose Garlands* (1506)
showing self-portrait

naught else but a father.' He clung to Pirckheimer and yearned for his pres-
ence. His letters are full of exclamations like 'If only you were in Venice!'
He spent days touring goldsmiths' establishments with experts, picking out
jewellery for his friend, sending him stones on approval and buying editions
of the classics and carpets on his behalf.

Work on *The Feast of Rose Garlands* took longer than anticipated, and
Dürer could have earned at least 200 ducats for other work in the same period.
He would gladly have taken his fifteen-year-old brother Hanns with him as
an apprentice, so that he could have assisted him and learned the language.
However, Hanns was something of a wastrel, and 'she (their mother) was
afraid lest the sky might fall in on him'. He brooded on what was happening
at home. On 2 April he wrote: 'And for my brother's sake tell my mother to
ask Wolgemut if he can make use of him and give him work until I come ...
Speak to the lad, as you so well can, and tell him to persevere in goodness
and honesty until I come. And let him not be a burden to his mother, for I
cannot do everything, though I do my best. I shall not come to grief myself,
but it is too hard for me to support many.'

Meanwhile, his fame and reputation was spreading through the city. 'Painters copy my work in the churches and wherever else they can find it.' The six small panels — oils on wood — which he had brought with him were all sold by this time, and one day the doyen of Venetian painters, Giovanni Bellini, visited him in his studio with the intention of inspecting his pictures and buying one. 'And everyone tells me that he is an upright, devout man, so that I am truly friendly with him. He is very old and still the best painter of all.' All annoyance at the envy of his Venetian colleagues — the men who also spoke ill of de'Barbari — deserted him at a single stroke. 'They say that, were he good, he would remain here.' However, Dürer himself remarked that 'there are many better painters here than Master Jakob is abroad', and he could not but laugh at the immaturity of his artistic taste and opinions during his first visit to Venice. 'And that which pleased me so well eleven years ago pleases me no longer; if I had not seen it for myself I should not have believed another.'

One can, incidentally, understand the envy of the Venetian painters, who saw a colleague from across the Alps, ringletted, cloaked, capped and elegantly bearded — a *pittore barbato* whose outward appearance caused them some amusement — snatch one of the year's richest commissions from their grasp.

Ground-plan and elevation of Dürer's lodgings in Venice. Drawing, 1506

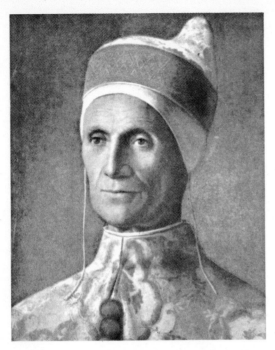

The Doge Leonardo Loredano
by Giovanni Bellini

Study for St Dominic in
The Feast of Rose Garlands (1506)

They had to admit, with a touch of irritation, that the excellence of his work was not confined to copperplate engraving. This he demonstrated in the 'little panels' which he had brought with him and in the portrait which he painted soon after his arrival — a young lady with silky golden ringlets, a red gown adorned with festive bows, and a sweetly sincere expression such as no native artist could have reproduced.

As a troublesome foreign competitor, Dürer had to be taxed. He was summoned before the Signoria three times and compelled to pay four gulden to the painters' school, or guild exchequer. He complained about this treatment in his letters. Indeed, his mistrust assumed such proportions that he gave credence to whispered rumours that a plot was afoot to poison him, and that he should avoid dining or drinking with other painters.

Dürer was in the midst of work on *The Feast of Rose Garlands* when he celebrated his thirty-fifth birthday. He had worked out the details in dozens of brush-drawings (of which only twenty-two are extant) done on blue-toned paper: portraits, drapery studies, hands, angelic figures, landscape views. Now he started to weld the parts into a whole. Despite his predilection for detail, which he had not abandoned, his work had lost its Gothic intricacy. There

Young Venetian Woman. Oils, 1505/06

was a merging of components, an assimilation of the graphic by the plastic, a subordination of line to mass. His shapes swung like a great bronze bell, clothed in enamel-like paints which glittered with the brilliance of jewels. Towards the end of August 1506, four months later than anticipated, *The Feast of Rose Garlands* was finally completed.

About a century after it was painted, Emperor Rudolph II, a fanatical Dürer collector, acquired the panel from the parish of San Bartolomeo. He had it packed in rugs and waterproof canvas and transported from Venice to Prague on carrying-poles. His collection was dispersed during the Thirty Years' War, however. Dürer's painting lay in a loft for decades before being nailed over a dormer window, where it remained undiscovered for decades more. The battered picture came to rest in the Strahow Monastery near Prague.

On completing the picture, Dürer wrote Pirckheimer some bumptious, idiotic letters in German-Italian gibberish, releasing the pent-up tension of the past months in flippant imbecilities, calling his friend a 'silk-tail' who spent his whole time running round after whores and was not half as pleasant to look at as he, Albrecht Dürer. He railed at old cronies in Nuremberg — 'riff-raff', as he called them — because they were probably making dirty jokes about their friend in the Venetian cesspit. No, no, he could not leave yet. He must earn some money first, and besides, he wanted to enjoy life. 'My French mantle and my Italian coat send you their regards', he wrote, verbally strutting up and down in front of his friend like a peacock. He even took dancing lessons, but soon dropped them because his dancing-master was appallingly expensive.

Meanwhile, Dürer's altar-piece had become the talk of all Venice. Painters, connoisseurs and patrons from the German colony swarmed into his studio. The Doge Leonardo Loredano came to inspect the new work accompanied by Domenico Grimani, Patriarch of Aquileia, both of them leading Venetian art connoisseurs. Dürer wondered whether to remain in Venice and accept a post as painter to the Signoria. An annual retainer of two hundred gulden would have banished all his financial worries. He asked for time to consider, but eventually declined the offer.

Dürer would have liked to accompany the Emperor on his journey to Rome (the Venetians had refused to grant him access to the mainland via their territory, much to the Germans' rage) and also to Padua, home of the aging Andrea Mantegna. It was Mantegna who had been his youthful example and whose engravings had first introduced him to classicism. Equally, Mantegna was anxious to meet the young and celebrated German.

The plan never materialized. When Dürer set off for Bologna at the end of October 1506 'to learn the secrets of the art of perspective, which someone is willing to teach me', it was already too late. Mantegna had died on 13 September at the age of seventy-five.

Dürer rode to the city at the approaches to the Apennines via Ferrara. In Bologna he was welcomed by his young fellow-townsman Christoph Scheurl, who was in the process of graduating from Bologna University. The artists' colony of the city, headed by Francesco Francia and Lorenzo Cossa, gave a banquet in honour of 'the new Apelles'. They called him the best painter in the world and declared, a trifle extravagantly, that 'they would die the happier for having seen Dürer, for whom they had yearned for so long'. However, Dürer had already enjoyed a surfeit of honours in Venice. His goal was the man with the 'secret of perspective', possibly Fra Luca Pacioli, teacher and friend of Leonardo da Vinci, who had supplied the figures for his treatise *De divina proportione*. Dürer was still tormented by the same old problem, the quest for a canon of beauty, coupled with a quest for accurate spatial representation as conveyed by perspective.

The miracle of artistic creation is not like a mathematical sum, though the Renaissance often thought so and attempted to prove it. Dürer, too, was impressed by this theory of art, but at the end of his life he was still confronted by the same unsolved enigma. 'What beauty is, I do not know . . .'

Kein ding hilfft für den zeitlichen Todt/
Darumb dienent Gott frü vnd spott.

1510

Das mög wir all wol erspehen	Do entfleucht keiner dem Richter nit
Das bald vns ein mensch ist geschehen	Durch allein du fürchtest hie Gott
Das so wir heut ein mensch haben	Dardurch entrinst dem ewigen tod
Vileicht wirt er morgen vergraben	Drumb heb an nach Christo zuleben
Darumb O mensch lich herckeit	Der kan dir ewites leben geben
Warumb sind dir nit dein sünd leyd	Des hals kain zeytlichs dinc an sich
So du doch wol hilft vernemen	Aber noch künfftigem richt dich
Das Gott all böß würt beschemen	Vnd thu stets noch gnaden werben
In ewikeit durch sein streng gericht	Als soltestu all stund sterben

Death and the Lansquenet
(1510) incorporating figure
of Albrecht Dürer

Title-page from Pacioli's
De divina proportione,
Venice 1509

Diuina
proportione

O pera a tutti glingegni perspi
caci e curiosi necessaria Oue cia
scun studioso di philosophia:
prospectiua pictura gsculptu
ra: Architectura: Musica: e
altre Mathematice: sua
uissima: sottile: e ad
mirabile doctrina
consequira: e de
lectarassi cō va
rie questione
de secretissi
ma scien
tia.

M. Antonio Capella eruditiss. recensente:
A. Paganius Paganinus Characteri
bus elegantissimis accuratissi
me imprimebat.
Joannis Alberti Vindruestadij
cognomento Lucretij .S.35.

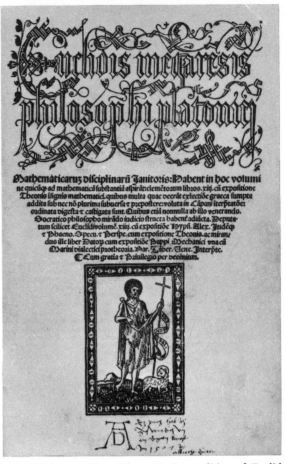

Detail from Giulio de Campagnola's fresco in the
Scuola del Carmine, Padua, showing portrait of Dürer

Title-page from Johann Tacinus' edition of Euclid,
Venice, 1505

Dürer's note on the title-page of this edition of Euclid: 'I bought this book for
one ducat in Venice in the year 1507. Albrecht Dürer'

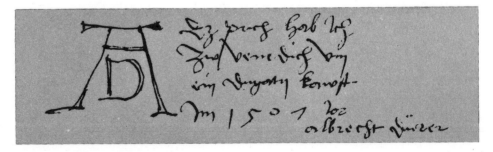

Christ among the Doctors.
Oils, 1506

After a few weeks he returned to Venice via Padua, where he may have seen Campagnola's mural in the Scuola del Carmine, which embodied a full-length portrait of Dürer himself. Back in Venice, he painted some more portraits and completed *Christ among the Doctors,* for which he had made studies while still at work on *The Feast of Rose Garlands.* The piece took only five days to complete, and he was so proud of his speed that he noted the fact on the picture. The general impression is that of a painted sketchbook sheet filled with grotesque 'types' of the kind which Dürer had seen among Leonardo da Vinci's drawings.

Before leaving for home, Dürer painted a stately German merchant's wife. The portrait had a formal delicacy, lack of metallic hardness and a mellow Venetian quality absent in other examples of his painting. He also acquired an early edition of Euclid's *Elements,* hoping to find in it an answer to the problems of mathematical laws and formal harmony which had been troubling him afresh ever since his visit to Bologna. He inscribed the purchase price and his monogram on the title-page, together with the date, 1507. Then it was time to leave the city which had honoured him like a great man and given him the happiest days of his life. In a last letter to his friend he wrote: 'How I shall freeze after this sun! Here I am a gentleman, at home a parasite.'

Extract from a letter to Pirck-heimer dated 13 October 1506

Hands of an Apostle. Study for the *Heller Altar-piece,* 1508

In February 1507 Dürer left Venice and rode home to Nuremberg. Seventeen months' absence in the South had been too long for some people. Art patrons were eager to share in his fame by acquiring new works, and Frederick the Wise ordered a *Martyrdom of the Ten Thousand Christians*. Dürer was still toiling over this exacting work with its multitude of tiny, mostly nude figures — in the midst of which he inserted two rather forlorn likenesses of himself and Pirckheimer — when he received a commission for an altar-piece depicting *The Assumption of the Virgin* from Jakob Heller, the Frankfurt merchant. 'I prefer not to undertake too many things at once, lest I become out of sorts', he wrote in reply. It was not until spring of the next year that he started on the panel, which he proposed to make so sound and beautiful 'that it will remain bright and fresh for five hundred years'. The Elector was paying him only 280 gulden for the *Martyrdom* — too little, Dürer considered, for the drudgery it entailed.

Head of an Apostle. Study for the *Heller Altar-piece*, 1508

Dürer was almost invariably engaged in disputes over fees. He was not avaricious; on the contrary, he sometimes verged on extravagance. He was quick to give things away, squandered money thoughtlessly on trifles which caught his fancy, gambled and lost or remitted his patrons' gambling debts, yet he never entirely lost his *petit bourgeois* fear of not being able to make ends meet. With true German conscientiousness, he always put more time and effort into his work than had been allowed for in the fee when the contract was drawn up — hence his frequent complaints that he would actually be losing money by completing a commission. In Jakob Heller's case there was a notorious and shameful exchange of letters in which Dürer repeatedly stressed his goodwill while simultaneously grumbling at the unprofitability of the contract. Finally, after receiving an arrogant and unsympathetic response from the Frankfurt business man, he lost patience and declared the contract void, instructing his banker, Imhoff, to return the deposit of 100 gulden. At this, Heller backed down and paid a revised fee of 200 gulden instead of the 130 stipulated in the original contract.

Only a copy of the altar-piece has survived, together with some twenty elaborately finished preliminary sketches of individual figures, heads, hands, feet and portions of drapery which Dürer, following his established procedure, put together to form the final picture like pieces in a jigsaw puzzle. Among them are the famous *Hands of an Apostle*. He slaved away at the picture for

Dürer's house in Nuremberg, showing city walls and Tiergärtnertor ▶

Dürer's Wife, 1510. Study for
St Anne in the painting
Virgin and Child with St Anne

thirteen months, while his assistants, who by this time probably included Hans Baldung Grien, worked on the wings. Dürer found 'donkey-work' exceedingly irksome. Reflecting that if he had confined himself to engravings since his return he would have been at least 100 gulden to the good, he decided to revert to engravings and woodcuts. Agnes, who had spent weeks selling drawings at Frankfurt Fair in the autumn of 1506, while he was still in Venice, had returned with a large profit.

However, fresh demands were made on the new celebrity's time — demands which he could not evade. The Nuremberg patrician Matthäus Landauer, a wealthy foundry-owner, wanted an All Saints altar-piece for the *Zwölfmännerhaus*, an old people's home which he had endowed. Once again, Dürer had to produce a multi-figured composition, but for the time being he confined himself to making a cursory sketch which kept his patron happy.

Dürer buys
a house
For the moment, Dürer was preoccupied with other worries. He proposed to buy a house, perhaps because life with his brothers in their parents' house

in Burgstrasse had become too irksome. He had been able to pay off a mortgage on his return from Italy, and probably felt that he had now done enough for the family. He planned to take his mother with him into the new house, which stood beside the Tiergärtnertor, immediately below the castle. This large corner-house at the mouth of Zistelgasse had formerly been occupied by the astronomer Bernhard Walther, a pupil of Regiomontanus. His observatory was still installed in the attic, but his heirs were anxious to get rid of it. Dürer put down 275 gulden in cash — about half the purchase price — and gradually paid off the remainder in the form of mortgages. Shortly afterwards he spent another 90 gulden on a large garden in front of the city gates, near the Little Church of St John. He moved into his new abode equipped, as he noted in his journal, with 'fairly good household effects, good clothes, some good pewter table-ware, good tools, bedding, chests and cupboards, and paints worth more than 100 Rhenish gulden'. This house, the *Dürerhaus* known to the world at large, has been restored. Despite bomb-damage, reconstruction and

Kitchen in Dürer's house

restoration, visitors to the house below Nuremberg Castle still find themselves bathed in the aura of Albrecht Dürer's genius.

Widely travelled, famous, owner of an imposing house, friend of the city's celebrated scholars and mathematicians, protégé of the Elector of Saxony and soon to be that of the Emperor, Dürer was now co-opted into the municipal administration of Nuremberg. In 1509, the year in which he purchased his house, he became a 'Nominee of the Grand Council'.

Refusing to abandon his engraving plans, he got his godfather Koberger to install a printing-press on the ground floor of his new home and established his workroom on the floor above. At the same time, he brought his work for Landauer, which was proceeding slowly, with him. The panel for the chapel of the old people's home was not to be a large affair — barely five feet high — but Dürer designed a frame incorporating pillars and a canopy ornamented with figures which formed part of the over-all composition. He had observed while in Italy how the architectural richness of a frame can harmonize with the picture it surrounds. In his picture, too, the arrangement of the earthly and heavenly choirs which hover

View from the window in 'the large chamber' in Dürer's house

'The small chamber',
showing Dürer's place of work

Entrance hall on the ground
floor of Dürer's house

The Holy Trinity. Woodcut, 1511   *Adoration of the Trinity by all the Saints*
(Landauer Altar-piece), 1511

amid clouds, worshipping the Trinity, is echoed in the frame and the canopy
embellished with sculptured figures. The keystone of the composition is an
ellipse, visible above as a semi-ellipse, into which — as into the celestial domain — only the heads of the Emperor and Pope protrude. The picture has
three horizons. The earthly horizon at the foot, which includes a section of
landscape and a self-portrait of the artist on the extreme right, holding a
signature plaque, joins the Celestial domain and the central area occupied by
adoring saints in forming a circle whose focal point is situated in the clouds
at the foot of the Cross.

While still engaged on this altar-piece, Dürer tackled *The Holy Trinity*,
a large woodcut. The 'donkey-work' was over at last, and his printing-press
on the ground floor worked unceasingly. New editions of *The Apocalypse*,
The Life of the Virgin and *The Great Passion* appeared, complete with title-
pages and a few additional engravings (1511). The popular *Little Passion*
(thirty-seven woodcuts) and the so-called '*Little*' *Copperplate Passion*, a work
intended for connoisseurs and collectors rather than the general public, appeared
at almost the same time. The goldsmith-like delicacy of Dürer's engrav-

Landauer Altar-piece without frame

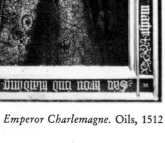

Emperor Charlemagne. Oils, 1512

Emperor Sigismund. Oils, 1512

ing technique increased, while his woodcuts became as substantial as paintings and his drawing acquired new flexibility. In *The Holy Trinity* he constructed his groups out of plastic masses bathed in light, so that the surface of the print, 40 centimetres high, was dominated by a gradation between light and shade. Many decades later, El Greco was to use it as a pattern for his great altar-piece in San Domingo el Antiguo at Toledo.

Dürer could not, of course, decline a commission which required his services as a painter. The imperial city of whose council he was a member asked him to produce two portraits — *Emperor Charlemagne* and *Emperor Sigismund* — destined for the adornment of the Chamber of Reliquaries in the Schopper

Emperor Maximilian. Charcoal drawing, 1518

family's house, where the imperial treasures were housed and exhibited publicly for one day in every year. These two idealized portraits, incorporating
coronation regalia and an accurate reproduction of the imperial treasures,
had to be delivered in 1512 because Emperor Maximilian was due to pay
Nuremberg an official visit. It was this which provided the occasion for
Dürer's first encounter with Maximilian — an encounter arranged by Willibald Pirckheimer, who was the Emperor's adviser on humanist questions. As
a successor of Charlemagne, Maximilian, 'the last of the knights' and an up-
holder of the fine arts, felt himself to be heir to the Holy Roman Empire and
the German nation. Although his political day-dreams were foundering on

VLRICHVS VARNBVLER ZC.M.DXXII.

Ulrich Varnbüler
(Chancellor to Emperor Maximilian).
Woodcut, 1522

the inauspicious climate of the times and his own weakness, he was determined to perpetuate himself and his regime at least in the realm of art. A tomb adorned with numerous figures cast in the Empire's many foundries, that of Peter Vischer of Nuremberg included, began to take shape in the Court church at Innsbruck. Maximilian now recruited Germany's most distinguished painter and draughtsman into a team of artists who were to devise him a 'triumphal arch' and 'triumphal car'. The triumphal arch never materialized save as a print measuring some eleven feet by nine, and the triumphal car was likewise engraved on wood and printed on paper, the Emperor's costly and abortive military operations in Italy — the Fuggers therefor advanced him a fortune — having left him no money to spare for marble and stone. Dürer, Cranach, Altdorfer, Burgkmair and other artists were obliged to comply with the Emperor's wishes and design components under the direction of his architect and Court painter, Jörg Kölderer of Innsbruck. It was

*Southern Hemisphere of
the Celestial Globe.*
Woodcut, 1515

From the marginal drawings in
Emperor Maximilian's Book of Hours, 1515 ▶

said that Maximilian ran a 'fame factory', for he commissioned a whole series of other curiosities, all of which
turned out to be artistically unsatis-
factory — if only because of the con-
sciously humanistic programme that inspired them.

Nevertheless, Dürer felt honoured at
this opportunity to work for the Emperor. As a citizen of an imperial city,
he saw the Emperor as a symbol of
unity, admired the Habsburg monarch
deeply and — like all who came into
contact with him — fell under the spell
of his personality. For all that, he enjoyed producing something a little light-
er and less inhibited, while in the service of his lord and master, than the
desiccated allegories of the triumphal
arch and car. In *Marginal Drawings for
Emperor Maximilian's Book of Hours*
his pen roamed across the parchment
pages laden with red, green and violet
ink, tracing figures which blended humour
with gravity. Dürer's 'inward wealth of
imagery' gushed forth in full spate.

It may be assumed that Dürer belonged

to the Emperor's more intimate artistic circle. His friends included Stabius, Maximilian's astronomer and historian, and Varnbüler, his chancellor. By dint of rendering them small favours (he drew the former's coat of arms and astronomical charts and made several portraits of the latter), Dürer ultimately succeeded in persuading Emperor Maximilian to sign a document, given at Innsbruck in 1515, assuring him of an annual pension in the sum of 100 gulden. The city of Nuremberg was instructed to pay this *Leibgeding*, or life-annuity, out of municipal taxes on the Emperor's behalf. Dürer, who had always been prone to financial worries, now saw his future assured. His expenditure of time and effort on things which he considered to be of doubtful value had borne fruit at last.

Enhancement and perfection were Dürer's goal, particularly in respect of his artistic life — hence his struggles with proportion, human anatomy and perspective, and hence the plastic style of drawing which he brought back with him from Italy. He had also acquired a new style of painting whose intensity, when set beside the serenity of Venetian works, occasionally lapsed into garishness.

The 'Meisterstiche' Burin in hand, Dürer brought the inherent potential of copperplate engraving to an acme of technical perfection during these years. His three 'Meisterstiche', or masterly engravings — *The Knight, Death and the Devil, Melencolia* and *St Jerome in his Study* — represent the *non plus ultra* of copperplate technique. These symbolic pictures, which originated in the years 1513 and 1514, are venerated with quasi-religious fervour in Germany. They

Study for *The Knight, Death and the Devil*. Water-colour, 1498

The Knight, Death and the Devil. Copperplate, *1513*

permit the beholder to see himself reflected, in turn, as a knight *sans peur et sans reproche,* a Faustian brooder, and a serene and enlightened sage.

Although these engravings did not come into being as components of a common programme, they have an inner affinity, and Dürer generally disposed of them in sets of three. Conceived four years before Luther posted up his Theses in Wittenberg, Dürer's Christian knight represented a symbol in the spirit of Luther's 'and were the world filled with devils...' His burin was now capable of expressing everything: smoothness, hardness, the warmth of cloth, the texture of material objects — even colour, which can be sensed in the tonality of his hatching. Engraving had entirely superseded his earlier water-colours.

Great speculation has always surrounded the print known as *Melencolia I,* though the significance of the inscription on the outspread bat's wings may be: 'Begone, dull care!' The dark angel, a genius crowned with laurel, gazes meditatively into space surrounded by a meaningless jumble of tools and implements. Mathematics, logic, Nature — all have lost their value. Life is holding its breath while the sand in the hour-glass trickles away. The *Faust* quotation 'and see, we can know nothing' is almost audible as one looks at the engraving, in whose magic square (top right corner, next to the passing-bell) can be deciphered the date of Dürer's mother's death, written in symbolic form.

Dürer was deeply affected by his mother's death, which evidently occurred while he was engaged on *Melencolia.* Two months earlier he had made a life-size charcoal drawing of her, a strikingly ugly portrait imbued with a sense of decay, dissolution and death, bitterness and mute uncertainty. Dürer added the date of her death subsequently. Writing in his journal, he described her death in ponderous, clumsy words strung together into the unwieldy, stumbling sentences typical of contemporary speech and writing. For all that, his account is as powerful as anything written in German at the time.

'Now you must know that in the year 1513, on a Tuesday before Rogation week, my poor afflicted mother, whom I took into my care two years after my father's death, since she was quite poor, after she had been with me nine years, one morning fell sick so suddenly that we broke into her chamber, for we should not otherwise have got in, she being unable to open to us. Accordingly, we carried her into a room beneath, and she was given both Sacraments, for everyone believed she would die... More than a year after the day on which she fell sick, in the year 1514, on a Tuesday, the seventeenth day of May, two hours before nightfall, my devout mother, Barbara Dürer, passed away Christianly, with all the Sacraments, absolved from torment and sin by Papal authority. She first gave me her blessing and wished me divine peace, with many a noble injunction to guard against

Melencolia. Copperplate, 1514

Dürer as a Sick Man.
Pen-drawing and water-colour.
'Dürer's handwritten note above
the figure reads: 'Where the yellow
patch is and I am pointing with
my finger, there it hurts me'

sin ... And she was mightily afraid of death, but she said that she had no fear of coming before God. Moreover, she died hard, and I marked that she saw something dreadful; for she asked for holy-water, though she had remained silent for a long time. I saw, too, how death dealt her two great stabs in the heart, and how she closed her mouth and eyes and passed away in pain. I prayed aloud for her. This grieved me more than I can express. God be merciful to her.'

The only escape from *Melencolia,* which conveyed the uncertainty of all existence, was to the quiet abode of wisdom and devotion. *St Jerome* was not only the last of the three engravings but also, Dürer implied, a symbol of the ultimate phase in human life.

By now, Dürer himself had reached a watershed, sensing, perhaps, that death was not so very far away. *Dürer as a Sick Man,* a full-length self-portrait in the nude, may date from this period. It shows him pointing at his spleen and bears the legend: 'It hurts me there.' The sensitive area on his abdomen is ringed in black.

Nevertheless, Dürer was not yet ready to retire to the 'abode of wisdom', but experienced a new and splendid prime during which his art and personality underwent their ultimate development.

1526.
VIVENTIS·POTVIT·DVRERIVS·ORA·PHILIPPI
MENTEM·NON·POTVIT·PINGERE·DOCTA
MANVS

Philipp Melanchthon. Copperplate, 1526

On 31 October 1517, Luther affixed his Theses to the door of the Schlosskirche at Wittenberg. They met with an overwhelming response throughout Germany, including Nuremberg, where humanist circles hailed Luther as a restorer of the Church and the true faith. Among those who associated with Pirckheimer and, later, Dürer, was Philipp Melanchthon of Wittenberg, *praeceptor Germaniae* and founder (at Nuremberg) of Germany's earliest grammar-school, which took his name. Central figure in the new movement at Nuremberg was Lazarus Spengler, the town clerk and a friend and neighbour of Dürer. Being in constant touch with towns in Southern Germany and Switzerland, Spengler received a stream of reports about religious innovations and unrest there.

Luther crossed Dürer's path intellectually, though not in person, on his trip to the Diet of Augsburg, where he debated with Cardinal Cajetan. The Diet had been convened by Emperor Maximilian. By now an old and weary man who was witnessing the collapse of the established order, Maximilian had gone into complete retirement and was writing his *Theuerdank,* a romanticized account of his youth. In June 1518 he sat for Dürer in a little room in the imperial palace. However, Dürer had not made the journey from Nuremberg solely for the sake of this portrait. The eyes of all Germany were focussed on Augsburg, and speculation mounted as to how the new developments would end. Dürer's ambition to meet Luther and make a portrait of him was never fulfilled, neither at Augsburg nor at *Dürer visits* any other juncture during the remaining ten years of his life, but it may *Zürich* have been his encounter with the 'Protestants' assembled there from Germany and Switzerland that prompted him to visit Zürich.

At the beginning of the following year, the old emperor who had granted Dürer his life-annuity died at Wels. Apprehensive about his future and worried by the prospect of old age, the artist wrote a letter to the city council on 27 April 1519, requesting that his pension be continued. Having pledged the house in Burgstrasse in case the new emperor declined to honour his predecessor's obligation, he set off for Switzerland without waiting for an answer. During the past few months he had been sending prints of his finest engravings and woodcuts to Luther in Wittenberg, including *The Knight, Death and the Devil,* a symbol of Lutheran courage in the face of death and evil. Dürer visited Switzerland at the invitation of the Swiss painter Hans Leu, who had studied under him a few years before. At Zürich he saw friends with whom he had discussed religious matters in Nuremberg, among them Felix Frey, and he also met the lay priest Ulrich Zwingli, whose sermons in the Minster were causing popular unrest.

Constructional studies of heads from the Dresden Sketch-book, 1519

He returned home after a few weeks. Since his letter to the city council had evidently failed to produce the desired effect, he had to prepare for another long journey. This time he proposed to visit the Netherlands in order to obtain confirmation of his life-annuity from Emperor Charles V, Maximilian's youthful successor. The city of Nuremberg was planning to send a deputation to the coronation at Aachen to deliver the imperial regalia, and Dürer could have travelled with it. Instead, he decided to turn the trip into a full-scale expedition, taking his wife Agnes and a young maidservant with him. He filled trunks and bales with household supplies sufficient for many months and packed his entire stock of copperplate engravings and woodcuts, both sets and individual prints, not omitting to put in his painting materials, sketching sheets, silverpoint pencils and charcoals. His diary, two copies of which have survived, gives a succinct and laconic account of the journey, of his receipts and expenditure, acquaintanceships and sight-seeing tours. Other entries record the names of his sitters, the sums spent on *pourboires,* the price of roast chicken, wine, overnight accommodation, eye-glasses and young stallions. Banquets and dinner parties, gambling debts, the cost of hot baths in Aachen, the price of clothes, headgear and gloves bought on

Journey to the Netherlands

The Scheldt Gate at Antwerp. From the Netherlands Sketch-book, 1520

Agnes Dürer and a Girl from Cologne. Silverpoint drawing
from the Netherlands Sketch-book, 1520

behalf of ladies back home in Nuremberg — nothing is omitted from the
Tagebuch der Niederländischen Reise, which covers the years 1520–21 and
renders them the most fully documented portion of Dürer's life.

Dürer and his companions left Nuremberg on 12 July 1520. Every village
they passed through, every stopping-place is mentioned. Their first halt was
Bamberg, where Frau Agnes wanted to make a pilgrimage to Vierzehnhei-
ligen. Dürer went to pay his respects to the bishop and asked him for a
Freibrief, or free pass, which would exempt him from paying duty on his
goods. He presented the bishop with a painted Madonna and prints of his
Apocalypse and *Life of the Virgin*, together with sundry other engravings.
In return, he got his letter of exemption and three letters of introduction
which stood him in good stead during his passage down the Main to Frankfurt and beyond. More than a score of entries referring to the Main passage
read: '... and I showed my pass, and they let me proceed.' At Frankfurt his
old patron Jakob Heller, for whom he had painted the altar-piece depicting
The Assumption of the Virgin ten years before, welcomed him by sending
a gift of wine to his inn. From there onwards the customs officers grew less
accommodating. At Bacharach and Kaub, for instance, Dürer had to make a
written declaration that he had no 'common merchandise' with him and would

View of Bamberg from the *Tucher Altar-piece*

'Apple goblet' based on a design by Dürer

either pay the toll or present a free pass within two months.

The Dürers disembarked at Cologne, where they visited cousin Niklas, who had served his apprenticeship with Dürer's father in Nuremberg decades before. The Cologne cousin no longer called himself Dürer, but 'Unger', in deference to his family's Hungarian origins.

At Antwerp Dürer took lodgings with Jobst Plankfeldt and waited for Maximilian's daughter, Margaret of Austria to grant him an audience which might help him in the matter of his life-annuity. It was she who had brought up the new emperor, her nephew, and she lived in Mechlin. The large commercial centre on the Scheldt reminded Dürer of Venice, whose far-flung connections with Arabia und the East were matched by Antwerp's with the New World via Spain and Portugal. Antwerp was the reshipment point for goods from all over Northern Europe and a place where agents for Portuguese business houses made vast fortunes out of their monopolies in overseas goods. Nuremberg and Augsburg merchants, too, maintained offices there. Dürer met fellow-countrymen who introduced him to useful contacts. He dined, wined and gambled with them, drawing their portraits or presenting them with prints from his inexhaustible store of engravings in return for favours received. The artists of Antwerp, headed by Quentin Massys, heard of his arrival and honoured their famous colleague with an official banquet. Recalling the occasion and the honours conferred on him, Dürer waxes quite verbose: 'And on Sunday, it was St Oswald's day, the painters invited me to their guild-hall with my wife and maidservant. They had all things there, silver table-ware and other precious table-ware and very rich food. All their wives were also present. And, when I was conducted to table, the company stood on either side as though they were conducting some great lord. Moreover, there were among them persons of name and quality, all of whom showed me the utmost deference and bowed deeply. And they declared that they wished to do all that was possible to do to please me . . . And so we made merry together, and it was far into the night when they escorted us home right honourably with lanterns.'

Dürer consorted with the leading Flemish painters throughout his stay in the Netherlands, among them Quentin Massys, Barent van Orley, Court painter to the Regent Margaret, Lucas van Leyden, who came from Holland and fell completely under Dürer's artistic influence, and, last but not least, his compatriot Joachim Patinir. The latter lent him paints and assistants, invited him to his wedding and, figure-work not being his forte, exchanged a landscape for four *Christoffel* (St Christophers) in various poses, for use as references. Dürer was greatly intrigued by the shrewd, intelligent, youthful features of Margaret's Court painter, whom he drew in charcoal and later painted. *Barent van Orley* is one of his finest portraits.

Through the Fuggers, Dürer came into contact with Portuguese and Italian merchants. He quickly struck up friendships with them, and his favourite table-companions were Bombelli, the Regent's paymaster, and the Portuguese factors ('Portugales') Jakob Brandon and Roderigo Fernandez, whom he presented with prints. To Fernandez he dedicated the so-called *St Jerome* which now reposes in Lisbon Museum. This picture was based on the drawing known as *Head of an Old Man*.

Emperor Charles' coronation was scheduled to take place at Aachen in October. The deputation from Nuremberg would be in attendance, and many of the Antwerp business community were travelling there for the occasion. Out of the blue, Dürer was summoned to Brussels for an audience with the Regent. It is probable that he got an opportunity to present his petition, backed up by a gift of his best engravings, but Margaret offered him no great encouragement on the subject of his life-annuity. On 4 October he left Flanders to attend the coronation at Aachen, where he admired and made drawings of the *Minster* and *Townhall,* watched the pomp and splendour of the coronation ceremony, assiduously visited the hot springs, lost many a *stuiver* gambling with his fellow-countrymen, and drew the three delegates from Nuremberg, *Groland, Ebner* and *Schlauderspach,* with whom he celebrated a bibulous reunion. However, none of this swelled his coffers, so he

Barent van Orley (Court painter to Margaret of Austria, Regent of the Netherlands). Oils, 1521 ▶

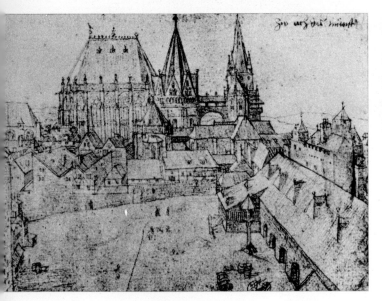

Aachen Minster. Silverpoint drawing, 1520   *Elector Frederick the Wise.* Copperplate, 1524

joined the Emperor's vast retinue and travelled from Aachen to Cologne, having left his wife and maidservant in Antwerp. Once again, 'my lords of Nuremberg' acted as his hosts. He witnessed the great coronation banquet at Gürzenich and the Princes' Ball, and visited his cousin Niklas once more. Finally, on 12 November, 'after great trouble and labour', he received the Emperor's *confirmacia*, or confirmation of his pension. Travelling back up the Rhine by boat, he rejoined his wife and their landlord, Plankfeldt, ten days later, bringing the completed document with him: 'Whereas the late and most illustrious Prince, Emperor Maximilian, Our beloved lord and grandfather of praiseworthy memory, granted and assigned unto Albrecht Dürer, trusty and well-beloved servant of Ourselves and the Empire ... We therefore earnestly command and require that you ... bestow upon and render unto the said Albrecht Dürer the life-annuity of one hundred Rhenish gulden ... CAROLUS.'

While in Cologne, Dürer had also visited the famous shrine of St Ursula and gained access to Stephan Lochner's *Adoration of the Magi*, now in Cologne Cathedral but then housed in the Rathaus. (It was this entry in Dürer's diary which led to the identification of the picture by art historians in the nineteenth century.)

Now that the official object of his journey had been achieved, Dürer felt at liberty to relax. He had made repeated trips into the country during his

Head of an Old Man.
Study for *St Jerome.*
Brush-drawing, 1521

Document dated 4 November 1520
relating to the confirmation of Dürer's
life-annuity by Emperor Charles V
(signed 'Carolus')

first weeks in Antwerp, inspecting churches, town-halls, castles, works of art and curiosities. Now, it appears, he embarked on as comprehensive a tour as possible. He viewed works by Rogier van der Weyden, Hugo van der Goes and Hans Memling at Bruges and Brussels, inspected Michelangelo's marble Madonna at Bruges and the van Eyck brothers' altar-piece in St Bavon's at Ghent, 'a most exquisite painting and well conceived, especially Eve, Mary and God the Father'. The painters of Bruges emulated their Antwerp colleagues by holding a banquet in his honour, after which he was again escorted home by torchlight.

In an endeavour to keep Dürer in Flanders, Antwerp offered him an annual retainer of 300 Philippsgulden (about £ 400) and a 'well-constructed house' if he would become painter to the city council. As he had in Venice fourteen years earlier, Dürer declined 'on account of the particular love and affection which I have borne toward this esteemed city (Nuremberg) and to my native land.'

It was well into December when Dürer paid a visit to Zealand to inspect an immense whale stranded there, an excursion which gravely affected his health. Travelling to Bergen op Zoom on horseback, he proceeded from there by boat, almost drowning in a stormy sea while trying to land. By the time he eventually reached his destination the whale had been washed away by the tide. Meanwhile, Dürer had fallen sick. 'And, formerly, when I was in Zealand, I was struck down by a wondrous sickness, the like of which I have heard no man relate, and this sickness I have still.' From then on, there was a steady increase in the number of entries in his diary relating to doctors' and apothecaries' bills. It is assumed today that the 'wasting disease' which gradually consumed Dürer and afflicted him with bouts of fever was malaria, which was rife in Zealand at this period.

When the new year came, Dürer's thoughts turned to departure. He dispatched a succession of bales to Imhoff in Nuremberg, some of them filled with the most bizarre assortment of articles — buffalo-horns, fish-fins, coral, Indian feathers, caps, porcelain vases, twelve pairs of gloves, bolts of silk, large nuts — all things which he had purchased or been given. Other items which he had been keeping in his Antwerp lodgings for months, e. g. tortoises, monkeys and parrots, had regretfully to be left behind.

Towards Easter, after Dürer had suffered another severe bout of fever and several fainting-fits, news reached Antwerp of the supposed murder of Luther, whose three recently published tracts, among them *The Freedom of a Christian Man,* had unleashed a storm of controversy there. Rumour had it that he had been assassinated while returning from the Diet of Worms. Dürer was profoundly shocked, and the entry in his journal, normally so dry and matter-of-fact, reads like a cry uttered from the depths of distress and despair. 'The

Erasmus of Rotterdam,
Copperplate, 1526

God-inspired man who delivered me from great terrors is dead!' His out-pouring of grief covers many pages. 'O God, if Luther be dead, who will expound the holy Gospel to us so clearly henceforth?' Then his thoughts turned to the shrewd and subtle scholar Erasmus of Rotterdam, whose portrait he had twice drawn during his time in Flanders. Perhaps this man, still one of Luther's adherents, was the man chosen by Providence. 'O Erasme Rotteradame, where will you tarry? Hear me, knight of Christ, ride forth beside the Lord Christ, attain the martyrs' crown!'

Now that the Emperor had decided against Luther at Worms, the Wittenberger's supporters in Flanders realized that measures would soon be taken against them. The sky over Europe darkened, and the religious wars which were to dominate politics and wreak devastation for a century loomed on the horizon.

Now anxious to get back to Nuremberg, Dürer was granted a farewell audience with the Regent Margaret. He intended to present the late Emperor's daughter with the portrait of her father which he had made at Augsburg, perhaps the last portrait the Emperor ever sat for, but she was so critical of it that — he concluded laconically — 'I took it away again.' He was permitted to inspect her art collection before he left, having previously been

Dürer's last years

able to see Cortez' Aztec treasures, which happened to be on display in Flanders at the time. Next, he paid farewell visits and exchanged parting gifts. Further bales were despatched to Nuremberg. Finally, with his packing complete and departure only a week away, he was invited to attend a banquet given by the exiled King Christian II of Denmark, who wanted him to do his portrait. The Emperor, the Regent Margaret and the Queen of Spain were also present. Next day, 13 July 1521, Dürer left Brussels for Nuremberg via Cologne. His sojourn in the Netherlands was at an end — and not before time. On the day of his departure, the first Protestants were arrested in Antwerp.

Dürer was actively engaged as a portraitist until the day he left the Netherlands. He drew hundreds of people in a single year, either because he liked their faces, or because he wanted to oblige his hosts, or — sometimes — to avoid giving a gratuity. His pencil moved with lightning speed, and his dexterity and sureness of touch verged on the miraculous. This facility is illustrated by an anecdote from Italy relating to a painters' competition in which a difficult problem had to be solved in the shortest possible time. Drawing free-hand round a central point, Dürer described a circle which subsequent examination with a compass proved to be perfect. He won the prize.

In taverns, on board ship, visiting friends or wherever else an interesting face caught his eye — Dürer always had paper and pencil at hand. He did not manage to do much painting during these unsettled and eventful months, but his portrait drawings acquired such a degree of

The Four Apostles, left-hand panel
(SS. John and Peter). Oils, 1526

rounded characterization that they may be regarded as portraits proper. It was typical of
Dürer's perfectionism and concentration that
his interest became increasingly confined to the
most fascinating subject and intriguing landscape in the world: the human face. Dürer's art
graduated from the outward and external to
the inward and spiritual. His new theme was
the face as a mirror of the soul. Although he
never permitted physiognomical accuracy to in-
terfere with artistic form, the process of dis-
covery and creation mattered more to him than
the finished product. Recklessly, he sold his
sketches for a song, gave them away or bartered
them for absurd pieces of bric-à-brac because
they no longer meant anything to him. Familiarity with hundreds of human faces had helped
him to acquire a knowledge of every nook and
cranny of the subject which was to occupy him
from now on. The Netherlands had served as
a training ground, a reservoir whence he could
derive material for the great works of his last
years.

The main items to have survived from the
closing years of Dürer's life are a few portraits.
Everything he undertook after his return either
remained at the planning stage or was destroyed
soon after, e. g. his *Virgin with Saints* for Riga
Cathedral, which was painted in 1523 and burnt
by iconoclasts two years later. His most famous work, *The Four Apostles* of 1526 (interpreted by some as 'the four temperaments'),
goes far beyond mere portraiture and embodies
the sum total of his knowledge of man as a
repository of the spirit. Dürer also left memo-
rials to five distinguished men who crossed his
path in the form of five engraved portraits:

The Four Apostles, right-hand panel
(SS. Mark and Paul). Oils, 1526

SS. John and Peter (detail from plate on p. 114)

SS. Mark and Paul (detail from plate on p. 115)

Erasmus of Rotterdam, the cool-brained scholar; his patrons *Frederick the Wise* and *Cardinal Albrecht of Brandenburg*, his friends *Willibald Pirckheimer* and *Philipp Melanchthon*. There is something genuinely monumental about these portraits with their inscribed plaques or backgrounds. They speak a language which has the simplicity and grandeur of classical coin portraits or marble reliefs.

It may be that art and the act of creation had lost some of its importance for Dürer. Aware, perhaps, that his days were numbered, he wanted to preserve what he knew about art and pass it on to others. 'For the arts are quick to disappear, but difficult and slow to rediscover.' This sentence from the dedication of *Underweysung der messung mit dem zirckel und richtscheyt* ('Instruction in measurement with compass and ruler'), addressed to his friend Willibald Pirckheimer, was the maxim governing all the theoretical work which he undertook during his last years and even on his death-bed. *Underweysung*, published by Koberger in 1525, was a summary of all the experience he had gained since his first encounter with art, of all that he had learnt from Mantegna, from antiquity, from Italian theories on art, from Vitruvius and Euclid. His aim was to provide German artists with a course of instruction in geometry, proportion and perspective which would prevent their going astray and save them the quest which he himself had undertaken, 'for nothing is more unpleasing to the right-minded than errors in

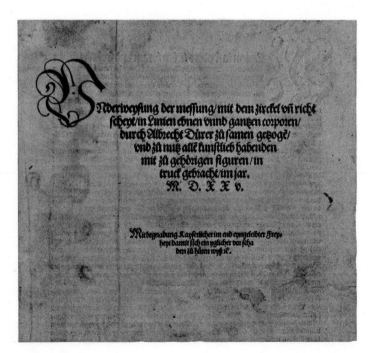

Title-page from *Underweysung der messung mit dem zirckel und richtscheyt*, Nuremberg, 1525

B ILIBALDI · PIRKEYMHERI · EFFIGIES
· AETATIS · SVAE · ANNO · L · iii ·
VIVITVR · INGENIO · CAETERA · MORTIS ·
· ERVNT ·
M · D · XX · iV ·

Willibald Pirckheimer.
Copperplate, 1524

painting.' German art, he declared, was like 'a wild unpruned tree', and a
man could only become a true master 'through the art of mensuration'.

Dürer greatly cherished the drawings which Raphael had sent him in 1515,
a gesture which he reciprocated by sending him a self-portrait, no longer
extant. What had come naturally to the Southerner, the artist rooted in the
soil of antiquity, Dürer determined to procure for German art by a system
of rules. He was never perturbed for a moment by the thought that, once
diverted into the narrow channel of rationalism, the stream of inspiration
loses its original spontaneous force. To him, standard laws were more impor-
tant to art than talent or inspiration.

Refusing to abandon art to the whim of the moment, Dürer insisted on
certainty, not only in shape and proportion but in faith. Whether tirelessly
pursuing research into proportion or immersed in Luther's writings, truth was
his invariable preoccupation. The modern conception of artistic licence would

Raphael: two nude studies for *The Naval Battle of Ostia,* and a study of a head

have evoked nothing but head-shaking from him. Indeed, he would probably have regarded such an attitude as godless and immoral. The older he grew, the more he conceived of art as a means of proclaiming something. Thus, in his last great work, the *Apostles,* he breaks into speech by having religious admonitions inscribed beneath the four figures, much as Beethoven condensed music into words in the last movement of his Ninth Symphony.

It was typically German of Dürer that, just when the ultimate had been attained and the supreme message was to be proclaimed, words had to intervene as deputies for and enhancers of visual form because the latter had become an inadequate medium of expression. To Dürer, the passages from Luther's translation of the New Testament, which he personally selected and got the calligrapher Neudörfer to inscribe beneath the Apostles' figures, formed the picture's real message.

The size of his figures was merely intended to underline his appeal to the conscience of his fellow-citizens. Religious controversy inside Nuremberg

Dürer's covering letter of 6 October 1526
referring to his presentation of *The Four
Apostles* to the city council of Nuremberg

had become debased. Dürer's pupils, Pencz and the two Behams, the 'godless painters' who renounced Christianity, were brought to trial and banished
from the city. *The Apostles,* which Dürer presented to the city council, was
his way of professing what he felt to be true. At the same time, he expressed
his thanks to them:

'Prudent, honourable, wise, dear Masters! Although I had intended, for a
long time past, to present Your Wisdoms with some unworthy painting as
a remembrance, I was constrained by the imperfection of my unworthy
works to refrain, being sensible that I could not well stand before Your
Wisdoms with the same. However, having of late painted a panel upon which
I expended more diligence than on other paintings, I consider none more
worthy to keep it as a remembrance than Your Wisdoms . . . I shall endeavour
in all humility to serve Your Wisdoms well. Nuremberg, October 1526. Your
Wisdoms' humble servant, Albrecht Dürer.'

During the previous year the council had accepted a loan of 1000 gulden

from him. The five per cent interest payable on this, added to the Emperor's life-annuity, was more than enough to provide for Dürer's old age. (In 1538, shortly before her death, Frau Dürer used the money to endow a foundation for theological students at Wittenberg University in her husband's memory.)

Apart from *The Apostles*, Dürer painted two other portraits — *Holz-schuher* and *Muffel* — which give the impression of being individual studies for the fully realized characters portrayed in *The Apostles*. Both men were burgomasters of Nuremberg at this period and must have been personally responsible for accepting Dürer's gift, for which the council subsequently paid him a further 110 gulden.

Everything Dürer did after his return from the Netherlands conveys a feeling that he was setting his affairs in order, that he sensed the imminence of his death. He refrained from superfluous activities and concentrated on essentials. He had completed one treatise and told his fellow-citizens what he had to tell them. His treatise on proportion was under way, and he proposed to write another manual for the budding painter entitled *Speis der*

Dürer's Vision. Pencil drawing and water-colour, 1525, bearing a written explanation by Dürer

Hieronymus Holzschuher, burgomaster of Nuremberg, aged fifty-two. Oils, 1526

*Malerknabe*n ('Food for Apprentices'). While engaged in sifting material for this, he suffered repeated attacks of fever. Filled with foreboding, he dreamt that he witnessed the end of the world, and committed his dream to paper next morning with a still trembling hand. *Dürer's Visio*n is of the unleashing of all natural forces and of the destruction of the world — a vision which, in the atomic age, has preserved much of its cogency.

'In the year 1525, during the night between the Wednesday and Thursday after Whit Sunday, I saw this vision in my sleep. Many great waters fell from the sky, and the first smote the earth about four miles from me with great ferocity, with an exceeding great roar and spray, and engulfed the whole land. I was so sorely terrified at this that I awoke before the other waters fell. And the waters that then fell were very great. Some of them fell far away, some nearer, and they descended from such a great height that they seemed to fall with equal slowness. But, when the first deluge to smite the earth came close, it fell with such swiftness, wind and roaring, that I was so terrified that I awoke, that my whole body trembled, and it

was long before I came to myself again. But when I arose in the morning I painted it above, just as I had seen it. May God turn all things for the best. Albrecht Dürer.'

Meanwhile, war had broken out between France and Germany. Peasant hordes were ravaging the country-side and the Turks had already reached the plains of Hungary. Now was the time to turn the towns into islands of security in a sea of unrest. Dürer had been interested in the art of fortification ever since the days when he saw the Venetian fortress of Arco above the road by Lake Garda. He now embodied all that he had seen recently in the Netherlands in his *Unterricht zur Befestigung der Städte, Schlösser und Flecken* (Nuremberg 1527). This treatise on fortification he dedicated to King Ferdinand I, whose imperial brother had entrusted him with the Habsburg territories in Germany and whose first task was destined to be the fortification of Vienna.

By now, disease had reduced Dürer to a skeleton. He was 'parched as a bundle of straw', Pirckheimer reported, and had abandoned all work save on his treatise on proportion, whose publication he still hoped to see. He completed sundry forewords and dedications to Pirckheimer, wrote re-drafts

Erhard Schön: *Portrait of Albrecht Dürer* at the age of fifty-six. Woodcut

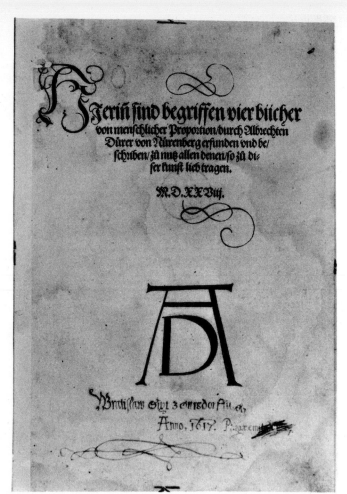

Dürer's last receipt in respect of his
life-annuity, dated 12 November 1527

Title-page from
Treatise on Proportion,
Nuremberg, 1528

and amendments and dictated corrections. The last surviving document in his handwriting is a receipt addressed to the city in respect of his life-annuity. It bears his seal. 'I, Albrecht Dürer, citizen of Nuremberg, publicly acknowledge on my own and my heirs' behalf that the prudent, honourable and wise burgomasters and councillors of the city of Nuremberg, my gracious masters, have willingly paid me the 100 Rhenish gulden assigned to me from the common city taxes of Nuremberg by the late Emperor Maximilian of most praiseworthy memory, which 100 gulden have fallen due this St Martin's day in this year... In token whereof I have affixed my seal to the foot of this my bond. Given the twelfth day of the month of November in the year 1527. Your Wisdoms' humble servant, Albrecht Dürer.'

Early in 1528 Dürer received the first proofs of his *Treatise on Proportion*, which he continued to correct on his death-bed. He died on 6 April, leaving behind a mass of handwritten notes for *Speis der Malerknaben*. The *Treatise*

Ich albrecht dürer Burger zu nörnberg Bekenn offentlich hiemit
für mich vnd meine erben, das mir die fürsichtigen Ersamen vnd
weisen Burgermeister vnd rate der stat nörnberg, mein gonstige herren,
die hundert gulden zinßlich So mir weilant keiser Maximilion
hochloblichster gedechtnus, auf der gewöntlichen stattstewr daselbst zu
nörnberg verschafft hat, welche hundert gulden zu dem Jetzigen Sannt
martins tag die jar zerfallen sind, gutwillig entericht haben,
Sag darum gedachter Burgermeister vnd rat als alle jr nachkumen
solcher hundert gulden vnd aller bißher bezalten vnd mir zu gebürigen
zeiten, Jn der pesten form für mich vnd mein erben, gentzlich quit
ledig vnd los, Zu bekant hab Jch mein eigen Sigill zu ende dieser
meiner hanntgeschrifft, hie auf getruckt Geben den 12 tag des
monats november Anno · 1 5 2 7 ·

Euer weisheit

vndertheniger
Albrecht dürer

on Proportion, a work destined to perpetuate Dürer's fame as an art theoretician for well over a century to come, was published posthumously by friends. New editions continued to appear: German in 1528, Latin in 1532–1534, French in 1557, Italian in 1591, Portuguese in 1599, Dutch in 1622, and English in 1660. Pirckheimer composed a funeral oration in Latin, as did Eobanus Hesse, who also spoke over Dürer's grave.

Dürer was laid to rest in a plot belonging to his parents-in-law, the Freys, in Nuremberg's St Johannis cemetery. His headstone bears the world-famous 'A D' monogram and a Latin inscription composed by Pirckheimer:

Quicquid Alberti Dureri mortale fuit sub hoc conditur tumulo

('Whate'er was mortal of Albrecht Dürer is interred beneath this mound')

Agnes Dürer inherited about 1000 gulden, enough to keep her in comfort. Dürer's favourite pupil, Hans Baldung Grien, 'Grünhanns', begged a lock of his beloved master's hair.

Bronze plaque on Albrecht Dürer's grave, bearing an inscription composed by his friend Pirckheimer

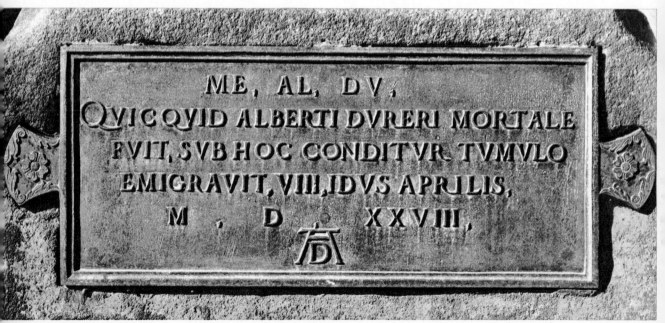

The St Johannis cemetery at Nuremberg, showing Dürer's grave ▶

ACKNOWLEDGEMENTS

The purpose of this book is to give a written and pictorial sketch of Dürer and his age, based on Dürer's personal testimony and that of his contemporaries. No complete coverage has been attempted, since it was the author's intention to present, not a text-book, but a universally comprehensible summary of the life and activities of Albrecht Dürer, the man and artist. The author would like to thank all who have assisted him in compiling this book, among them Professor Dr L. Grote of the Germanisches Nationalmuseum, Nuremberg; the Fränkische Galerie and the chairman of the Albrecht-Dürer-Verein, Nuremberg, Dr W. Schwemmer; W. Kriegbaum, Bildarchiv, Nuremberg; Dr Schnelbögl and Dr Hirschmann, Staatsarchiv, Nuremberg; Prof. Dr H. Kehrer, Munich; the Municipal Library, Nuremberg; the Kupferstichkabinett, Berlin; the British Museum, London; the Louvre, Paris; the Alte Pinakothek, Munich; Staatliche Graphische Sammlung, Munich; öffentliche Kunstsammlung and the Library of the University, Basle and the Albertina, Vienna. Last but not least, thanks are also due to my wife and children.

1471 21 May: 'Sixth hour of the day', birth of Albrecht Dürer at Nuremberg. Father: Albrecht Dürer the Elder, goldsmith. Mother: Barbara, née Holper, daughter of Hieronymus Holper, goldsmith of Nuremberg, from whom Dürer senior learnt his craft. Godfather: Anton Koberger, printer and publisher of Nuremberg.

1475 12 May: Dürer's father buys a house at the intersection of Schmiedgasse and Burgstrasse.

1481–82 Dürer attends St Lorenz grammar-school.

1483–86 Apprenticed as a goldsmith to his father.

1484 *Self-portrait* (silverpoint drawing). 25 April: birth of Dürer's brother Endres, later a goldsmith.

1486–89 Apprenticed as a painter to Michael Wolgemut. *Portrait of The Artist's Father* (silverpoint, 1486).

1490 *Portrait of The Artist's Father* (earliest extant oil-painting by Dürer). 21 February: birth of Dürer's brother Hanns, later a painter.

1490–93 Dürer visits Colmar and Basle (1491–92). *Self-portrait* (pen-drawing, 1491). *Self-portrait* (pen-drawing, 1492). *Self-portrait with Thistle* (oils, painted at Strasbourg in 1493).

1494 7 July: Dürer marries Agnes Frey at Nuremberg.

1494–95 First visit to Italy. Influence of Mantegna, Bellini and Pollaiuolo.

1495 February: returns to Nuremberg and establishes atelier in paternal home in Burgstrasse. Friendship with Willibald Pirckheimer.

1497 Dürer finally adopts 'AD' monogram as his signature. Elector Frederick the Wise of Saxony becomes his patron.

1498 *Self-portrait* (Madrid). Completes *The Apocalypse* and starts on *Life of the Virgin*. (Title-pages added to second editions of these series, Latin, 1511). Begins woodcut series known as *The Great Passion*.

1499 *Tucher Portraits* and *Portrait of Oswolt Krel*.

1500 *Self-portrait* (Munich), altar-piece depicting *Lamentation. Female Nude with ellipse of proportion.*

1501–04 Studies of plant and animal life.

1502 20 September: death of Dürer's father.

1504 *Adam and Eve*, first major fruit of Dürer's preoccupation with problems of proportion.

1505–07 Second visit to Italy. Through the good offices of Dr Peutinger, town clerk of Augsburg, Dürer is commissioned to paint *The Feast of Rose Garlands* for the church of the German colony in Venice. Correspondence between Dürer and Pirckheimer. Other paintings: *Madonna of the Goldfinch, Christ among the Doctors*. Drawings and portraits: *Venetian Woman, Wife of a German Merchant*, etc. May have met Leonardo da Vinci in Milan, also his teacher Luca Pacioli, whose *De divina proportione* was then in production.

1507 Dürer purchases edition of Euclid's *Elements*. February: returns to Nuremberg. Apprentices in Dürer's atelier include his brother Hanns and his most famous pupil, Hans Baldung Grien.

1508 Altar-piece commissions: *Martyrdom of the Ten Thousand Christians*. (Previous examples: *The Paumgartner Altar-piece* and *Adam and Eve*, Madrid.)

1509 14 June: buys house near Tiergärtnertor. Becomes a 'Nominee of the Council'.

1510 Koberger installs a printing-press on the ground floor of Dürer's new house. Dürer becomes his own publisher.

1511 Publication of second editions of his woodcut series: *The Apocalypse, The Life of the Virgin, The Great Passion, The Small Passion, The Copperplate Passion;* also *The Holy Trinity. The Coronation of the Virgin* (an altar-piece commissioned by the Frankfurt merchant Jakob Heller), and the *Landau Altar-piece (Adoration of the Trinity by all the Saints).*

1512 The Grand Council commissions Dürer to paint two portraits (*Emperor Charlemagne* and *Emperor Sigismund*) to decorate the Chamber of Reliquaries

in the Schopper family's house by the market, where the imperial regalia had been kept since 1424. Dürer buys a garden in front of the Tiergärtnertor 'by the seven crosses'.

1513–14 Copperplate engravings: *The Knight, Death and the Devil, Melencolia, St Jerome in his Study.*

1514 17 May: death of Dürer's mother. Studies in human proportion based on the canon by Leonbattista Alberti. *Dürer's Mother* (only surviving portrait).

1515 Collaborates on *Triumphal Arch* and *Triumphal Car*. Becomes friendly with Stabius, the Emperor's astronomer, and Ulrich Varnbüler, his chancellor. 6 September: the Emperor signs at Innsbruck deed granting Dürer a life-annuity of 100 gulden. Marginal drawings for the Emperor's Book of Hours.

1518 A gift from the Emperor enables Dürer to settle outstanding mortgage on his father's house in Burgstrasse. Drawing of the Emperor, made at the Diet of Augsburg.

1519 January: death of Emperor Maximilian. May–June: Dürer visits Switzerland, where he meets Ulrich Zwingli, the Swiss reformer. *Portrait of Emperor Maximilian I*. Adds note to *Portrait of Michael Wolgemut*. Death of Wolgemut.

1520 Journey to the Netherlands. The city council of Nuremberg refuses to continue payment of Dürer's life-annuity after Maximilian's death, compelling him to seek confirmation from Emperor Charles V. 12 July: sets off with wife and maidservant, reaching Antwerp on 25 August. Princely reception from painters' guild. Dürer draws *Erasmus of Rotterdam* and *Nikolaus Kratzer*, Henry VIII's Munich-born Court astronomer. September: audience with Margaret of Austria, daughter of Maximilian. Dürer gets to know numerous personalities – painters, business men, etc. – makes portraits of them and presents them with copies of his engravings. 23 October: travels to the Emperor's coronation at Aachen. Through the good offices of Frederick the Wise, finally obtains confirmation of his life-annuity by Charles V on 4 November. Declines tempting offer to remain in Antwerp. Excursions to Brussels, Ghent, Bruges and Zealand. Dürer falls ill.

1521 News of Luther's alleged death arrives at Whitsun. Dürer's appeal to Erasmus. Audience with the Regent. 12 July: departure for Nuremberg.

1523 21 November: death of Hanns Frey, Dürer's father-in-law.

1524 Dürer begins to write family chronicle and journal. 17 October: requests city council of Nuremberg to accept a loan of 1000 gulden at 5 per cent interest.

1525 Publication of *Underweysung der messung mit dem zirckel und richtscheyt* ('Instruction in measurement with compass and ruler').

1526 Dürer presents the city council of Nuremberg with the twin panels depicting *The Four Apostles,* his greatest work. Portraits in copperplate and oils include *Pirckheimer, Frederick the Wise, Erasmus, Melanchthon, Holzschuher* and *Muffel.*

1527 Publication of *Treatise on Fortification,* dedicated to Emperor Ferdinand. Dürer collects material for *Speis der Malerknaben,* but never completes the book. His physical condition deteriorates. He reads the first proofs of his *Treatise on Proportion* (published posthumously).

1528 6 April: death of Dürer.

Frontispiece: *Self-portrait* (detail) dated 1500. (Alte Pinakothek, Munich. Reproduction: F. Bruckmann KG, Munich).

5 *View of Nuremberg*, 1483. This view of the city, showing the Kaiserburg and the churches of St Lawrence and St Sebald, forms the background of the Krell Altarpiece in St Lawrence's. (Photograph: Bildarchiv, Nuremberg.)

6 *The Dürer Coat of Arms.* Woodcut, 1523. Open doors on shield refer to family name, also spelt 'Türrer' or *'Türer' (Tür* = 'door') in family chronicle.

7 *Dürer's birthplace.* Albrecht Dürer was born here on 21 May 1471. This house, which belonged to the Nuremberg lawyer Dr Johannes Pirckheimer, father of Dürer's lifelong friend Willibald Pirckheimer, was destroyed in 1944. (Photograph: formerly Staatliche Bildstelle, Berlin.)

8 *Astrological Drawing*, 1503–04. Possibly drawn for Dürer's friend Lorenz Beheim, who cast his horoscope in 1507. Astrology and astronomy were much in vogue during the Renaissance. Dürer was also a friend of Stabius, Court astronomer to Maximilian I, and drew astronomical charts for him.

9 *The 'Schöner Brunnen'* in the marketplace at Nuremberg. This fountain, which incorporates the figures of seven Electors, Moses, the seven Prophets and various pagan and Christian heroes, came into be-ing in the second half of the 14th century. Heinrich Parler, who was responsible for the chancel in St Sebald's, is assumed to have been its designer. (Photograph: Bildarchiv, Nuremberg.)

10 *Albrecht Dürer the Elder.* Silverpoint drawing made in 1486, while Dürer was learning the goldsmith's craft from his father. It is unsigned, and some authorities consider it to be a self-portrait by Dürer the Elder. (Albertina, Vienna.)

Letter from Albrecht Dürer the Elder to his wife, dated 1492. Dürer's father worked as a goldsmith for Emperor Frederick III. (Germanisches Museum, Nuremberg.)

11 *Dürer's Mother*, Barbara, née Holper. Charcoal drawing, 1514. (Kupferstichkabinett, Berlin.)

12 *Enrolment of Endres Dürer*, Albrecht's brother, as a master-goldsmith in the official city records of Nuremberg for 1514. Endres Dürer (1484–1555) took over his father's workshop. (Photograph: Staatsarchiv, Nuremberg.)

Endres Dürer. Portrait drawn by Albrecht in 1514, when Endres, then thirty, became a master-goldsmith. (Albertina, Vienna.)

12 *Dürer's paternal home.* In 1475, when Dürer was four years old, the family moved from Winklerstrasse to Burgstrasse. Dürer was later apprenticed to Michael

Wolgemut, who lived two doors away. (Photograph: Bildarchiv, Nuremberg.)

13 *Hanns Dürer,* Albrecht's youngest brother. (Albertina, Vienna.)

14 *Earliest Self-portrait,* made at the age of thirteen. Silverpoint drawing. (Albertina, Vienna.)

15 *Michael Wolgemut.* Dürer, who painted this portrait of his former master in 1516, entered his atelier as an apprentice in 1486. (Germanisches Museum, Nuremberg.)

Nuremberg Castle. Detail from one wing of the altar-piece in St Jacob's, Straubing. Principal work of Michael Wolgemut, *c.* 1475. Photograph: Bildarchiv, Nuremberg.)

View of Nuremberg, showing imperial forest. This water-colour, now in the possession of the Germanisches Museum, Nuremberg, dates from 1516.

16 *Nikolaus Cusanus' Map of the World* (1491). Detail showing Central Europe from North Sea coast to Adriatic. (Germanisches Museum, Nuremberg.)

17 *Madonna in a Courtyard,* one of the most famous engravings by Martin Schongauer (1445–91). Dürer hoped to learn the art of copperplate engraving from him. (Photograph: Braun, Munich.)

18 *Self-portrait* on the back of a sketching-sheet, showing the young Albrecht Dürer looking into a mirror, Pen drawing. (University Library, Erlangen.)

19 *The Temptation of St Anthony,* by Martin Schongauer. It is probable that Matthias Grünewald, who used similar mythical beasts for his Temptation of St Anthony in the Isenheim Altar-piece, was familiar with Schongauer's engraving. (Staatliche Graphische Sammlung, Munich.)

20 *Self-portrait with Thistle* (1493) may have been painted as a betrothal gift for Agnes Frey. It is now in the Louvre, Paris. (Photograph: Preiss, Munich.)

21 *Christ-Child with Globe,* dated 1493 and signed 'A D'. Tempera on parchment, 11,5 x 9,8 cm. (Albertina, Vienna.)

22 *View of Basle.* While Dürer was travelling in the Upper Rhine area and Switzerland, Koberger published *Schedel's Chronicle of the World* (Nuremberg 1493), from which this woodcut is taken. (Photograph: Germanisches Museum, Nuremberg.)

23 *St Jerome removing the Thorn from the Lion's Paw.* Original woodcut and print, the former bearing Dürer's name on reverse. While working as a commercial artist in Basle, Dürer probably produced actual engravings as well as working drawings. (Photograph: Öffentliche Kunstsammlung, Basle.)

Letter from Dürer to Amerbach dated 20 October 1507. Fifteen years after his stay in Basle, Dürer was still writing to his former employer in extremely affectionate terms. (University Library, Basle.)

24 *Self-portrait with Cushion.* Pen-drawing dating from 1493, when Dürer was travelling as a journeyman. (Lubomirski Museum, Lvov.)

25 *Earliest-known terrestrial globe,* made by the Nuremberg navigator Martin Behaim in 1490–92. (Germanisches Museum, Nuremberg.)

Map of the world from *Schedel's Chronicle of the World* (Nuremberg 1493), showing Europe, Africa and Asia. (Germanisches Museum, Nuremberg.)

26 *Lady of Nuremberg in Church-going Dress* and *Lady of Nuremberg in Ball-dress.* Water-colour, 1500. At the top of these sketches are the following remarks in Dürer's handwriting (omitted in our reproductions): 'Thus do folk go to church in Nuremberg' and 'Thus do the women of Nuremberg go to the dance'. (Albertina, Vienna.)

27 *Dürer's Wife.* This pen-drawing of Dürer's young bride Agnes, née Frey, dates from 1494–95 and bears the legend: 'My Agnes'. (Albertina, Vienna.)

28 *View of Venice.* Woodcut from *Schedel's Chronicle of the World,* Nuremberg 1493. (Photograph: Germanisches Museum, Nuremberg.)

29 *Detail from Etzlaub's Map* (1492), with cardinal points of the compass reversed. At extreme upper edge: Italy, showing Rome and Venice. Dürer's devious route from Nuremberg to Venice can be traced on this map. (Germanisches Museum, Nuremberg.)

30 *View of Innsbruck* from the north, showing Emperor Maximilian's castle and, in the background, the Patscherkofel. Water-colour, 1494. (Albertina, Vienna.)

31 *Courtyard of the Hinterburg at Innsbruck.* Dürer recorded this view in water-colour from two different angles. (Albertina, Vienna.)

32 *Nemesis* ('The Great Fortune'). Copperplate engraving of c. 1501 embodying a souvenir of Dürer's first trip to Italy. He used a drawing of Klausen (now Chiuso)

in the southern Tyrol as reference material for the landscape beneath the female figure hovering above the clouds. (Staatliche Graphische Sammlung, Munich.)

33 *View of Trento on the Adige*, recorded in water-colour during Dürer's first visit to Italy (1494–95.) Formerly in the Kunsthalle, Bremen, but missing since 1945. (Photograph: Albertina, Vienna.)

34 *Fashionably dressed Venetian Lady.* Profile and rear view on same sheet. Pen-drawing and wash, 1495. (Albertina, Vienna. Photograph: Hessische Treuhandverwaltung, Wiesbaden.)

Lobster, probably made at the fish market in Venice in 1495. Pen-drawing and tempera. (Kupferstichkabinett, Berlin. Photograph: Hessische Treuhandverwaltung, Wiesbaden.)

35 *The Whore of Babylon.* Woodcut from the *Apocalypse* series (1498), employing pen-drawing of a fashionably dressed Venetian woman made in 1495 (opposite).

36 *Virgin and Child.* Chalk drawing, 1518. Like other examples of Dürer's work which were formerly in Bremen's Kunsthalle, this drawing vanished during the post-war chaos. (Photograph: Braun, Munich.)

The Great Hercules, a copperplate engraving in which Dürer re-employed the female figure which appears on the left in *Orpheus Slain* (page 45). This engraving has been variously interpreted as 'Jealousy' and 'Chastity and Unchastity'. It also embodies figures taken from Mantegna and Pollaiuolo. (Photograph: Braun, Munich.)

37 *Jakob Fugger.* The bales of merchandise exported to Italy by the Fuggers and

Imhoffs also included engravings by Dürer. Jakob Fugger, whose portrait Dürer probably painted at Augsburg during the Diet of 1518, was Emperor Maximilian's financier. The Fugger family also controlled the sale of indulgences in Germany. (Alte Pinakothek, Munich. Photograph: Bayerische Staatsgemälde-sammlungen, Munich.)

38/39 *Bird's-eye view of Venice*, published by the Nuremberg cloth Merchant Anton Kolb in 1500, measures about four-and-a-half feet by nine. It is probable that Dürer worked on the drawings with Jacopo de'Barbari. (Photograph: Braun, Munich.)

40 *Sheet from a sketch-book* dating from Dürer's first visit to Venice includes sketches of the Rape of Europa, lions' heads, an Apollo with bow and arrow and a Mussulman with a skull. Pen-drawings. (Albertina, Vienna. Photograph: Braun, Munich.)

41 *Apollo*. This pen-drawing depicting the god in company with Diana, who is trying to shield herself from the sun's rays with raised arms, was modelled on an Italian engraving in which the figure of Apollo was taken from the classical sculpture known as the Apollo of Belvedere. (British Museum, London. Photograph: Braun, Munich.)

42/43 *Globe* drawn by Dürer in 1515 for his friend Johannes Stabius, Court astronomer to Emperor Maximilian. The wind-gods are reminiscent of those in Kolb's plan of Venice. Woodcut.

44 *Battle of Tritons* (1494), a pen-drawing based on a copperplate engraving by Mantegna. (Albertina, Vienna. Photograph: Braun, Munich.)

45 *Orpheus Slain by the Thracian Women* may be another pen-drawing copied from a work by Mantegna. Note the re-employment of the female figure which appears on the left in *The Great Hercules* (page 36). (Kunsthalle, Hamburg. Photograph: Braun, Munich.)

46 *The Fortress of Arco*. Water-colour probably painted by Dürer while passing the Venetian frontier stronghold north of Lake Garda on his return journey from Venice. (Louvre, Paris.)

47 *Study in proportion* from Leonardo da Vinci's *Canon of Human Proportion* (after Vitruvius) shows a male figure circumscribed by a circle and a square. The handwritten text is in mirror-script. (Academy, Venice.)

48 *Ornamental Knot* composed of endless lines, school of Leonardo da Vinci. Dürer copied similar knots and linear ornaments and later embodied them in his pen-drawings for *Emperor Maximilian's Book of Hours*. (Photograph: Steck, Prien/Chiemsee.)

48/9 *View of Nuremberg* in 1520. Water-colour by Hans Wurm. (Germanisches Museum, Nuremberg.)

49 *Willibald Pirckheimer*. Dürer made both charcoal and silverpoint portraits of his friend in 1503. This charcoal drawing is in the Kupferstichkabinett, Berlin. (Photograph: Braun, Munich.)

50 *Miraculous Cross*. During the plague epidemic of 1503, crosses are reputed to have fallen from the sky at many places. Dürer made this drawing of one which a neighbour's servant-girl found imprinted on her shift. (Kupferstichkabinett, Berlin. Photograph: Steck, Prien/Chiemsse.)

51 *The Doctor's Dream* (1497–99) ist supposed to represent Willibald Pirckheimer. (Photograph: Nationalbibliothek, Vienna.)

52 *The Apocalypse*, a series of fifteen woodcuts, appeared in 1498 in two editions, German and Latin. The title-page which formed the sixteenth sheet was not added until the second edition of 1511.

53 *The Four Horsemen of the Apocalypse* — Death, Famine, War and Disease — is one of the most famous woodcuts in the *Apocalypse* series, which Dürer signed with the final version of his 'A D' monogram. (Photograph: Staatliche Graphische Sammlung, Munich.)

54 *The Men's Bath*, a woodcut produced while Dürer was engaged on *The Apocalypse* (1497–98). In it, Dürer worked some studies in human anatomy into a figurative composition. (Photograph: Nationalbibliothek, Vienna.)

55 *St Michael fighting the Dragon*, a woodcut from *The Apocalypse* series, depicts monsters which recall Schongauer's engraving *The Temptation of St Anthony* (page 19). The landscape is thought to be reminiscent of the Lake of Constance. (Photograph: Braun, Munich.)

56 *Constructed Male Figure*, a pen-drawing dating from 1512. (Albertina, Vienna.)

57 *Hercules and the Birds of Stymphalis* (c. 1500). The figure of Hercules is derived from a work by the Italian painter Pollaiuolo. (Germanisches Museum, Nuremberg.)

58 *Studies for Adam and Eve* (page 59) constructed 'in proportion' with compass and ruler. (Photograph: Nationalbibliothek, Vienna.)

59 *Adam and Eve*. This copperplate engraving dated 1504 and inscribed 'Albert Durer Noricus faciebat' represents a preliminary synthesis of Dürer's intense preoccupation with the standing nude, male and female. (Photograph: Nationalbibliothek, Vienna.)

60 *Columbine*. Water-colour, c. 1502. Dürer studied and drew flora and fauna with great scientific interest. The date '1526' was added by another hand. (Albertina, Vienna. Photograph: Nationalbibliothek, Vienna.)

61 *The Owlet*. Like most of Dürer's nature-studies, this water-colour of 1508 is in the Albertina, Vienna.

62 *Virgin and Child with Animals* (1502–03). This pen-drawing includes a number of animal studies which Dürer re-employed in contemporary engravings, among them *Adam and Eve*. (Albertina, Vienna. Photograph: Nationalbibliothek, Vienna.)

63 *Oswolt Krel*, painted by Dürer in 1499, came from Lindau and was manager of the Ravensburg trading company. (Alte Pinakothek, Munich. Photograph: Staatliche Gemäldesammlungen, Munich.)

64/65 *The Dresden Altar-piece*, painted by Dürer between 1496 and 1499 for the Schlosskirche of his patron, Elector Frederick the Wise, at Wittenberg. These panels, which are in a very poor state of preservation, belong to Dresden Art Gallery but are at present being laboriously restored in East Berlin after eleven years' exile in Russia.

66/67 *Adoration of the Magi*, now in the Uffizi at Florence, was painted in 1504 for Elector Frederick the Wise of Saxony. (Photograph: Preiss, Munich.)

68/69 *The Paumgartner Altar-piece,* whose centre panel depicts the Nativity, was originally installed in the Katharinenkirche, Nuremberg. The small figures on the main panel, portraying the donor's family, were subsequently painted over and not uncovered again until 1903. (Alte Pinakothek, Munich. Photograph: Bayerische Staatsgemäldesammlungen, Munich.)

70 *Self-portrait* (1498) depicts the painter dressed as a young Venetian nobleman. (Prado, Madrid. Photograph: Preiss, Munich.)

71 *Self-portrait* (1500) probably passed into the possession of Nuremberg's city council on Dürer's death in 1528, and is now in the Alte Pinakothek, Munich. It bears the inscription: '*Albertus Durerus Noricus ipsum me propriis sic effingebam coloribus aetatis anno XXVIII*' ('I, Albrecht Dürer of Nuremberg, portrayed myself thus, in my natural colours, at the age of twenty-eight'.) (Photograph: Bayerische Staatsgemäldesammlungen, Munich.)

72 *The Life of the Virgin,* a series of twenty woodcuts, came into being between 1498 and 1510. The title-page, dated 1511, mentions Dürer's friend Chelidonius (Benedikt Schwalber), abbot of the Scottish Monastery at Vienna, as being author of the text.

The Great Passion, another woodcut series, also originated between 1498 and 1510 and contained some verses composed by Abbot Schwalber. The title-page dates from 1510.

73 *The Prodigal Son,* a pen-drawing of 1497–98, served as a pattern for the (reversed) engraving of the same period. (British Museum, London. Photograph: Nationalbibliothek, Vienna.)

Memento mei. This charcoal drawing of King Death on horseback was inspired by the plague epidemic of autumn 1505. (British Museum, London. Photograph: Braun, Munich.)

75 *The Feast of Rose Garlands,* a panel painted by Dürer for the church of the German business community in Venice, San Bartolomeo, in 1506, shows Pope Julius II and Emperor Maximilian praying before the Virgin. Apart from members of the German colony, the panel also portrays Dürer himself, Dr Konrad Peutinger, town clerk of Augsburg, and Hieronymus, master-builder of the new German Fondaco in Venice. (State Gallery, Prague. Photograph: Braun, Munich.)

76 *Hieronymus of Augsburg,* master-builder. Brush-drawing. (Kupferstichkabinett, Berlin. Photograph: Nationalbibliothek, Vienna.)

Self-portrait from *The Feast of Rose Garlands* is badly damaged. The panel was used to reinforce a dormer window during the 17th century. (Photograph: Prof. H. Kehrer, Munich.)

77 *Dürer's lodgings in Venice.* This architectural drawing of Dürer's shows the frontage, side elevation and ground plan of the house where he stayed. (British Museum, London. Photograph: Steck, Prien/Chiemsee.)

78 *Portrait of Leonardo Loredano* by Giovanni Bellini. The Doge was one of Venice's foremost art connoisseurs. (National Gallery, London. Photograph: Steck, Prien/Chiemsee.)

Study for St Dominic in *The Feast of Rose Garlands,* now in the Albertina, Vienna. In the actual painting, St Dominic is blessing a young priest, assumed to be a likeness of Cardinal Domenico Grimani of Venice, Patriarch of Aquileia. (Photograph: Nationalbibliothek Vienna.)

79 *Portrait of a Young Venetian Woman* must have been painted in autumn 1505, shortly after Dürer's second arrival in Venice. (Gemäldegalerie, Berlin-Dahlem. Photograph: Marburg.)

81 *Death and the Lansquenet.* Woodcut, 1510. Dürer also composed the poem that went with it.

De divina proportione by Luca Pacioli, Leonardo da Vinci's teacher and collaborator, whom Dürer may have visited in October 1506. (Photograph: Staatsbibliothek, Munich.)

82 *Euclid's Elements.* While in Venice, Dürer acquired the latest edition of this famous book. On the title-page of his copy he inscribed his 'A D' monogram and the words: 'I bought this book for one ducat in Venice. In the year 1507. Albrecht Dürer.' Library Wolfenbüttel.

Giulio Campagnola's fresco in the Scuola del Carmine at Padua incorporates a portrait of Dürer and was probably painted during the latter's second visit to Venice. (Photograph: Prof. Dr. L. Grote, Nuremberg.)

83 *Christ among the Doctors.* This picture was painted towards the end of Dürer's second visit to Venice. A slip of paper protruding from the book in the left foreground bears the legend: '1506 AD OPUS QUINQUE DIERUM' ('work of five days'). (Thyssen Collection, Lugano. Photograph: Nationalbibliothek, Vienna.)

84 *Hands of an Apostle.* Study for the hands of one of the praying Apostles in the centre panel of the *Heller Altar-piece,* possibly modelled on Dürer's own hands. Compare the hand in the Munich self-portrait of 1500. (Albertina, Vienna.)

85 *Head of an Apostle.* Brush-drawn study for the Apostle on the extreme right of the *Heller Altar-piece.* (Albertina, Vienna. Photograph: Nationalbibliothek, Vienna.)

86 *Dürer's Wife.* Dürer employed this drawing of his wife Agnes as St Anne (Albertina, Vienna) for the painting *Virgin and Child with St Anne* in the Metropolitan Museum, New York. (Photograph: Nationalbibliothek, Vienna.)

87 *Dürer's house* near the Tiergärtnertor, accurately reconstructed after sustaining severe bomb-damage in the last war. (Photograph: Bildarchiv, Nuremberg.)

88/9 *The interior of Dürer's house* still contains original items dating from the artist's lifetime. The basin and spherical kettle visible on the wall of the 'small chamber' figure in his drawings. (Photograph: Bildarchiv, Nuremberg.)

90 *The Holy Trinity*, a woodcut. El Greco used it as a model for his great altarpiece in Toledo's San Domingo el Antiguo almost a century later.

Landauer Altar-piece, with frame. The frame which Dürer designed for this altar-piece, also known as *Adoration of the Trinity by all the Saints,* is housed in the Germanisches Museum, Nuremberg. (Photograph: Nationalbibliothek, Vienna.)'

91 *Landauer Altar-piece,* panel only, showing what an integral part of the composition Dürer's specially designed frame represented. In the bottom right corner can

be seen a full-length portrait of the artist with a plaque bearing the inscription: ALBERTVS DVRER NORICVS FACIEBAT ANNO A VIRGINIS PARTV 1511 AD. ('Albrecht Dürer of Nuremberg made this in the Year of Our Lord 1511 after the Virgin Birth'). (Kunsthistorisches Museum, Vienna.)

92 *Emperor Charlemagne* and *Emperor Sigismund.* Dürer painted these two panels (just over six feet high) for the Chamber of Reliquaries in the Schoppersches Haus, Nuremberg 1512. (Germanisches Museum, Nuremberg.)

93 *Emperor Maximilian I,* a charcoal drawing made during the Diet of Augsburg in 1518. It bears Dürer's note: 'This is Emperor Maximilian, whom I, Albrecht Dürer, portrayed in his small chamber, high up in the palace at Augsburg, in the year 1518 on the Monday after John the Baptist.' (Photograph: Nationalbibliothek, Vienna.)

94 *Ulrich Varnbüler,* Chancellor to Emperor Maximilian I, was a friend of Dürer. The Latin inscription on this woodcut portrait made in 1522 records Dürer's wish to preserve Varnbüler for posterity.

Astronomical Drawing. This working sketch for Dürer's woodcut of the southern hemisphere of the celestial globe was drawn for his friend Johannes Stabius, Court astronomer to Emperor Maximilian. The inscription tells us that Stabius commissioned the work, that Konrad Heinfogel supplied the position of the stars, and that Dürer drew in the shapes of the constellations. (Photograph: Steck, Prien/Chiemsee.)

95 *Emperor Maximilian's Book of Hours* was printed on parchment at Augsburg

and adorned with marginal drawings by Dürer at the Emperor's behest. Some of the pages are now in Munich and others at Besançon. The Munich collection contains pages by Dürer and Lucas Cranach the Elder, while the remainder includes work by Hans Baldung Grien, Hanns Burgkmair, Jörg Breu and probably Albrecht Altdorfer. (Photograph: Staatsbibliothek, Munich.)

96/7 *The Knight, Death and the Devil* (copperplate, 1513). Dürer made use of an old water-colour (left) painted in 1498. It bears Dürer's handwritten note: 'Such was the armour in Germany at the time.' (Albertina, Vienna. Reproduction: F. Bruckmann KG, Munich.)

99 *Melencolia,* a copperplate engraving made by Dürer in the Year of his mother's death. (Reproduction: F. Bruckmann KG, Munich.)

100 *Dürer as a Sick Man.* Self-portrait bearing the words: 'Where the yellow patch is and I am pointing with my finger, there it hurts me.' Pen-drawing and water-colour made when Dürer was about forty-five years old and suffering from a spleen infection. (Formerly in the Kunsthalle, Bremen — whereabouts since 1945 unknown. Photograph: Steck, Prien/Chiemsee.)

101 *St Jerome in his Study* (1514). In this, the last of the three *Meisterstiche,* Dürer depicts a highly atmospheric interior which foreshadows the still-life quality of Dutsch 17th-century interior painting. (Photograph: Nat.-Bibliothek, Vienna.)

102 *Philipp Melanchthon* sat for this copperplate portrait while visiting Nuremberg in 1526, charged with reforming the educational system. The engraving's Latin

inscription states that, while Dürer may have managed to reproduce the outward appearance of his sitter, he has failed to capture his mind. (Photograph: National-bibliothek, Vienna.)

103 *Studies of Heads* constructed like mathematical bodies. The *Dresden Sketch-book* illustrates particularly well how Dürer evolved his plastic bodily shapes from stereometrical structures. (Landesbibliothek, Dresden.)

104/05 *The Scheldt Gate at Antwerp.* This pen-drawing, made during Dürer's visit to the Netherlands, bears the inscription '1520 Antorff' (the old name for Antwerp) and measures 21 × 28,3 cm. (Albertina, Vienna. Photograph: Nationalbibliothek, Vienna.)

106 *Agnes Dürer and a Girl from Cologne,* a silverpoint drawing made during the river-passage to Cologne. It is inscribed: 'My wife on the Rhine near Boppard.' Beside the girl's head, Dürer wrote: *kölnisch gepend* ('Cologne head-dress'). (Albertina, Vienna. Photograph: Nationalbibliothek, Vienna.)

107 *View of Bamberg.* Dürer's journey to the Netherlands began with a trip up the Main from Bamberg. The background of the *Tucher Altar-piece,* 1485 (on permanent loan from the Tucher family to the Germanisches Museum, Nuremberg) depicts the town of Bamberg, the Cathedral, the Obere Pfarrkirche and, dominating the scene, the Michelsberg.

Goldsmith's work. Nuremberg's Germanisches Museum owns an 'apple goblet', based on a late design by Dürer. (Photograph: Germanisches Museum, Nuremberg.)

109 *Portrait of Barent van Orley* in Dresden Art Gallery is also known as *Bernhard von Resten.* The sitter is holding a slip of paper bearing the words: *dem bernh . . . zw . . .* Dürer mentions that he painted Bernhard von Resten's portrait in his Netherlands Diary, and that he received eight gulden for his services. Many authorities connect this reference with the Dresden picture. (Photograph: Dresden Art Gallery.)

110 *Aachen Minster.* This view of the Minster was drawn from the coronation chamber during Charles V's coronation. (British Museum, London. Photograph: Steck, Prien/Chiemsee.)

Frederick the Wise (1524), copperplate engraving with inscription at base (not reproduced here). The Musée Bonnat at Bayonne owns a silverpoint version of this engraving dating from the same year. (Photograph: Nationalbibliothek, Vienna.)

111 *Head of an Old Man.* This brush-drawing on toned paper heightened with white served as a model for a St Jerome which Dürer presented to his friend Roderigo Fernandez, a Portuguese agent in Antwerp. The painting now hangs in Lisbon Museum. Dürer noted on the drawing: 'The man was 93 years old and still hale.' (Albertina, Vienna. Photograph: Nationalbibliothek, Vienna.)

Dürer's life-annuity. Dürer received Charles V's confirmation of his imperial pension at Cologne on 4 November 1520. Bottom left: the signature 'CAROLUS'. (Staatsarchiv, Nuremberg.)

113 *Erasmus of Rotterdam.* Dürer's copperplate engraving of the great scholar,

based on a charcoal drawing now in Paris, was made in 1526, six years after their last encounter. When Erasmus saw the print he wrote: 'Dürer has made my portrait, but it resembles me not at all.' The portrait was cut at the request of Erasmus himself, who wrote to Pirckheimer on the subject. (Photograph: Nationalbibliothek, Vienna.)

114/117 *The Four Apostles.* The city councillors of Nuremberg originally installed these two panels in the Losunger Stube in the Rathaus. A century later, in 1627, they handed them over to Maximilian I, Elector of Bavaria, who had Johann Neudörfer's inscriptions sawn off. Maximilian, a fanatical Dürer collector, commissioned the painter G. J. Fischer to make copies of the panels, to which the severed inscriptions were then attached. Being unable to prevent this exchange, the city council of Nuremberg had to leave the originals in Maximilian's possession. In 1922 the inscriptions and the old frames were reunited with the original panels in the Alte Pinakothek, Munich. (Photograph: Bayerische Staatsgemäldesammlungen, Munich.)

118 *Underweysung der messung mit dem zirckel und richtscheyt,* Dürer's first treatise on mathematics and the theory of art, appeared in 1525. It was dedicated to his friend Willibald Pirckheimer. (Photograph: Bildarchiv, Nuremberg.)

119 *Willibald Pirckheimer* was a man of fifty-three when Dürer made this copperplate engraving. (Photograph: Nationalbibliothek, Vienna.)

120 *Raphael* sent Dürer a set of drawings from Rome in 1515. In return, Dürer sent him a self-portrait (not extant). One of Raphael's drawings has survived. It bears the following note in Dürer's handwriting: 'Raffahel de Urbin, who is so highly esteemed by the Pope, made these nude figures and sent them to Albrecht Dürer in Nuremberg, to direct his hand.' (Albertina, Vienna.)

121 *Letter of Presentation* in Dürer's handwriting, dated early October 1526 and addressed to the city council of Nuremberg. It refers to the two panels known as *The Four Apostles,* which he presented to the city. (Staatsarchiv, Nuremberg.)

122 *Dürer's Vision,* an apocalyptic vision of the end of the world, sketched and described on a sheet dated 1525. (Albertina, Vienna. Photograph: Nationalbibliothek, Vienna.)

123 *Hieronymus Holzschuher* was burgomaster of Nuremberg when Dürer presented his *Apostles* to the city council. (Gemäldegalerie, Berlin-Dahlem. Photograph: Preiss, Munich.)

124 *Dürer's Treatise on Fortification* — full title: *Etliche underricht zu befestigung der Stett, Schloss und Flecken* — was dedicated to King Ferdinand I. (Photograph: Bildarchiv, Nuremberg.)

125 *Profile of Dürer.* In later years, Dürer wore his hair medium-length and straight. This woodcut by Erhard Schön, dated 1527, includes a simplified version of Dürer's coat of arms in the top left corner.

126 *Dürer's Treatise on Proportion,* which he continued to work on as he lay dying, appeared posthumously in 1528. (Photograph: Bildarchiv, Nuremberg.)

127 *Last surviving example of Dürer's handwriting.* This is a facsimile of the last receipt he issued in respect of his life-annuity, which fell due at Martinmas, 10 November 1527. It bears Dürer's seal at the foot. (Staatsarchiv, Nuremberg.)

128 *Bronze plaque on Dürer's grave* carries an inscription by Willibald Pirckheimer. (Photograph: Bildarchiv, Nuremberg.)

129 *The St Johannis cemetery at Nuremberg,* with Dürer's grave in the foreground. (Photograph: Bildarchiv, Nuremberg.)

INDEX OF NAMES

Page numbers in italics refer to pictures

*Index
of names*